Glade's J

Also by Pauline Kidner:

Life with Bluebell

My Secret World

Videos:

Badgers in My Kitchen

A Chance to Survive

All the above are available from:

PK Publishing
Secret World, New Road,
East Huntspill, Nr Highbridge,
Somerset TA9 3PZ
Tel. 01278 783250
Fax 01278 793109

Glade's Journey

Stories from
an Animal Hospital

Pauline Kidner

PK Publishing
SOMERSET

PK Publishing,
Secret World, New Road,
East Huntspill, Nr Highbridge,
Somerset TA9 3PZ

First published in the UK by PK Publishing, 1999

Sincere thanks is given to everyone who has helped with
the preparation of this book, especially to Margaret
Aherne, Heidi Cussons and Jason Venus and all
photographic contributors.

A copy of the British Library Cataloguing in Publication
Data for this title is available from the British Library.

ISBN 0 9536628 0 2

Contents

Dedicated to two people who, all through my life, have always been there for me, no matter when or why. Absence never changes our relationships, you are both special.

With love to my sister, June Millen, and my best friend, Sheena Brown.

Foreword

Andrew Lynford

Something very unusual happened to me recently. I had been appearing in the TV drama 'Eastenders' for three years, and when I announced that I was planning to leave for pastures new (one of the pastures being in Somerset as it turned out!) I was asked if I would like to present a new children's animal documentary series, 'Wild Thing'. I have always been a bit animal crackers – I had just made two major trips abroad working for the Born Free Foundation and the Environmental Investigations Agency – I agreed straight away. I received the scripts for the new show and looking through it, I saw we were to visit a place called 'Secret World'. 'What's that, then?' I asked the director, who had visited all locations prior to shooting. 'Oh, it's a wonderful place where this woman has transformed her home into a haven where badger cubs run around the kitchen, and fox cubs are nursed back to health, and barn owls fly down and sit on your shoulder, and there's even an albino wallaby hopping about the place . . .' I raised an eyebrow – after all, it sounded a bit far-fetched. Not exactly the wildlife parks and nature reserves we were also due to visit. But then I saw it for myself. And it was all true.

I spent the most extraordinary two days filming with Pauline and her incredible workforce. I never would have thought I'd bottle-feed a young badger cub, who would then suckle my finger as though I were his mother; have the hairs on the back of my neck preened by a barn owl; hold a tiny dormouse in the palm of my hand while he slept deeply during his hibernation; play tug-of-war with a young fox cub who knew more about playing to the camera than I did . . . the amazing list is endless.

But apart from the residents or guests from the animal world, the thing that really strikes you about 'Secret World' is the positive atmosphere. It is not often you are in a place where you can almost feel the joy that everyone has for working there. It is, of course, incredibly hard work. Baby badgers like to be fed a good few times through the night, you know! But all the volunteers and staff seem to be right behind Pauline and her endeavours, whether that means trying to get a stubborn red deer to bed or making the cakes (which are delicious by the way) for the tearoom as part of the daily routine. It is a shared commitment. Coming from a television background, it is quite a humbling experience. The next time I am getting stressed because my costume doesn't quite fit me, I'll remember that it isn't the end of the world! There are more important things to worry about – and the people at 'Secret World' are taking care of some of them. Usually as many as they can at any one time.

As you will soon find out by reading this book, Pauline has a wicked sense of humour. Sense of humour is often what keeps us going, and because of her slightly crazy existence it obviously helps Pauline from time to time. I was new to the presenting game, but Pauline had been interviewed so many times for so many different television programmes, she was the easiest person to work with on camera. It was a case of lighting the touch-paper and standing back! I didn't have to sweat too much about covering all the various points the producer had requested – Pauline would briefly ask me what the questions would be, and usually in one 'take' it would be dealt with! That was when we weren't giggling too much . . . or when she was trying to get future 'Eastenders' storylines out of me!

I am so honoured to have been allowed to become a small part of 'Secret World'. I am now a patron, and have made several more trips to the wonders just off the M5! I advise anyone who needs to breathe in some country air – and some new ideas about what dedication and commitment is all about – to visit the Bluebell Sett* at Secret World, and mingle with the creatures there (both human and animal!). And after reading this wonderfully warm book, I am sure you will.

July, 1999

Bluebell Sett is the registered charity that supports Pauline Kidner's work at Secret World.

1

Dog on the Roof

The aroma of evergreen filled the bottom floor of our old farmhouse as I started to decorate for Christmas. Ivy, holly and evergreens picked from the garden were piled high on the old flagstone floors ready to be put up with tinsel and garlands, so that all the visitors to our Badger and Wildlife Centre would join in our celebrations for the festive season.

The huge mantel over the inglenook fireplace always looked beautiful filled with greenery and draped with gold strands to accentuate the brass around the room. We also gather cones from many forests where our orphan badger releases have taken place through the years. Each year brings orphan badger cubs to our door, many so tiny that they have to be fed on bottles. Once weaned the small cubs are mixed in with family groups. Then it is time for them to be sent to grassed enclosures so that they will become wild before being released. Indeed, from the different kinds of cones, I can remember many things: the area which each family group went to, the names given to individuals, their personalities and the joy they gave to me in the short time that they were with us.

It was the beginning of December, when I was 27, that I came to this farm, now called Secret World, as a housekeeper to three young children and bringing a small son of my own. The years have seen a change from dairy farm to an open farm as a Visitor Centre, which, through our involvement with wildlife (especially badgers), has expanded to include casualty pens and a hospital room to cater for injured and orphaned wildlife.

It's hard to believe that the kitchen, still with the old Rayburn and lovely pine dresser, now serves as the tearoom kitchen to provide meals for over 50,000 visitors each year. The whole of the bottom floor three rooms, that had been playroom, lounge and lazy room, are now the farmhouse tearooms.

As I pinned the garlands on to the picture rail around the high-ceilinged room, the logs spluttered in the wrought iron grate that we had brought down from one of the bedrooms upstairs. One, as we know from its date stamp, was built in 1885 and I am reminded of the many changes that have taken place in this 300-year-old farmhouse since I came in 1975.

Derek, the farmer, and now my husband – long suffering as he is – has seen his home fill with animals and these days spends more time farming visitors than animals! Being mild mannered and having a good sense of humour has stood him in good stead for the ups and downs of our unusual lifestyle. Ordering goods for the shop, sorting out the advertising and doing all the paperwork that goes with employing over twenty people is a far cry from the time when he ran the farm on his own. And of course, who better to be Father Christmas, especially as his beard is somewhat greyer than when he first started being Santa, although he does still need a cushion to be able to portray the rounded figure (not such a big one though – it comes to us all!).

We try to keep Christmas as traditional as we can, and when the children come to see Father Christmas we tell them about the mammals that sleep through Christmas, missing having presents and everything! There are always plenty of hedgehogs at this time of year, making the most of the hotel service at our Centre and staying through until spring, having been brought in underweight for hibernation. So these are always the first animals to be shown.

2

Last year, as I gathered the children up for the talk, a very talkative three-year-old was very keen to tell me that all he wanted was 'a bell for my bike!'. 'Well, you can tell Father Christmas when we see him and I'm sure, if you have been very good, he will try very hard to make one for you', I told him. Satisfied with this, he joined everyone else for the talk in the Discovery Den – making sure he was right up the front and therefore the first to go through to the grotto. Arms folded, he was ready.

Wishing everyone a Happy Christmas, I explained that we were to see the animals first whilst waiting for Father Christmas to arrive. Reaching inside the cage by my side, I asked, 'Can you guess what I have in here? It's something that you – '

'Is it a bell for my bike?' the little boy piped up. Everyone laughed.

'No, you have to see Father Christmas for that', I replied. 'It's an animal that you might be lucky enough to find in your garden. One that normally sleeps through the winter but is very difficult to pick up because it's prickly.'

Hands shot up and a little girl at the back excitedly exclaimed that it was a hedgehog. It was a young juvenile hedgehog, and as it was used to being handled it was easy to see the small black beady eyes, with its wet rubbery nose busy scenting the air. I showed it to the visitors and explained that hedgehogs need to be over 500 grams to survive the winter. They were able to see how the hedgehog rolled up if held on its back and touched. Pulling the muscle that encircles its body like a drawstring on a bag, it is able to tuck its legs and head inside and become a complete prickly ball. The children – and adults – were fascinated, for although hedgehogs are common not many people get the chance to see them close up. Not Fred in the front – 'When's Father Christmas coming?' he asked.

'In a minute, but first we have another animal to look at', I said, trying to divert his attention. 'Can anyone think of a mammal – another one – that sleeps all through the winter – but this one, if you've read *Alice in Wonderland*, is the one that they keep putting in the teapot?' The children look excited and several are guessing what it is –

'A rabbit?' one child guesses.

'No, rabbits stay awake all through the year – that's because their food is available all the time and they don't need to sleep in the cold winter. – It's the only mouse that has a furry tail,' I say, giving them a clue.

A proud parent exclaims, 'A squirrel!'

'Er, no – you're right, they do have a furry tail and they are a rodent – but not a mouse', I said (quickly trying to think of a way of saying he'd got it wrong!). 'And then, they store their food so they don't need to hibernate although many people think that they do.'

'It's a dormouse', declared a young boy. His cheeks flushed when he realised that he was right. We keep dormice for a breeding programme for releasing the young back into areas where they have become extinct, and in December they are usually sound asleep. From their aviaries, where they are wrapped in a beautiful ball of moss and leaves, we are able to bring them in and let the children hold them – but only for a very short time as the warmth of their hands would soon wake the mice up. With their tail curled over their heads, they are perfect golden balls of fur and it is possible to hear them snore. Hard to believe that in the wild, they will sleep from November through to April, only waking in January to take pollen from catkins before returning to their long hibernation.

The children's faces glow in wonderment at the small whistling mammal in the palm of their hand. They have probably never seen these before: the small dormice with their eyes shut tight, their whiskers only just moving with the slow breathing. Everyone is fascinated, all except one: 'When's Father Christmas coming?' the little boy moaned.

Mum soothed him. 'I want a bell for my bike!' he exclaimed – the voice becoming louder.

Standing with tinsel round my neck, a flashing badge and antlers on my head, I was the soul of patience and said, 'Very soon, as we have only one more animal to see before we go to the grotto. This is the last mammal that hibernates, one that sleeps through the winter, as we only have three in this country that hibernate. But this one, although a mammal, can fly!'

'I want . . .' – his mother's hand slipped quietly over his mouth.

One little girl at the back had been enthralled by it all. She had loved the hedgehog and had thought the dormouse was wonderful, and was quite sure, from the clues that I had given, that she knew exactly which animal was going to be in this small box that I was holding up. It was a mammal and it could fly, and she was beside herself that she was going to see one. I nodded my head at her and said, 'What do you think it is?'

Whispering in suspense, she breathed: 'Is it a reindeer?'

Looking at the small box in my hand, my first thought was – why do I do this?! But gathering my thoughts I quickly replied, 'No, it's not – but then they are all far too busy to be here today. It is one of the smallest bats – a pipistrelle, which although it is less than 5 centimetres long and weighs hardly anything, will eat up to 3,000 insects in one night!'

Luckily, the little girl was just as impressed. For my part I was quite happy for it to have been a bat and not a reindeer, considering that they can be as much as 2 metres tall and weigh up to 320 kilos!

At last, having shown the bat to everyone, as Sarah our supervisor came in to show the visitors our barn owl, it was time to start taking children through in turn to see Father Christmas. Little Fred was up and by the door in a flash, with 'I want a bell for my bike' tripping off his tongue as he ran. His parents had my every sympathy as there were still two weeks to Christmas and I don't think this guy was going to be able to wait that long.

We usually show the children the sheep with the lambs in the pen by the grotto and talk about the animals at the manger, but Fred had no time for this! Taking him through to see Father Christmas, there was no worry that he would be shy – he was straight on Father Christmas's knee and explaining in great detail this bell that was required for his blue and yellow bike.

'A very cheap Christmas for Mum and Dad then!' joked Father Christmas, who then went on to explain that he was sure, as long as he had been a very good boy, that he would be getting lots of presents at Christmas. So today Father Christmas was going to give him a pack with a pot, some seed and fat, so that with the help of an adult he could make a fat bell for the birds to hang up in the garden on Christmas Eve, and then the birds would be able to have a Christmas dinner on Christmas Day just as his family would do. Carefully, Father Christmas gave him his present from under the branch laden with fairy lights and twinkling stars, and the little boy's face glowed.

Feeling very proud at being able to make a bell for the birds, little Fred climbed down from Father Christmas clasping his present in one hand and Mum's hand in the other. 'But,' he said, as he waved good-bye, 'you won't forget the bell for my bike!'

It is sad in a way, that the story of Jesus' birth is often forgotten in the razzmatazz of present-giving, and while they are waiting to go in to see Father Christmas, I often ask the children when we are by the ewe with lambs if they can remember which animals were by the manger. We have some Dorset sheep, which are the large chunky white sheep with horns that curl around the face, and each year we have been lucky enough for one to produce twins at the beginning of December. 'Can you see the lambs?' I would ask the children, pointing to the lambs lying quietly in the straw as the ewe was busy eating her hay. 'One is called Tinsel and one is called Cracker. The shepherds brought Jesus a lamb, didn't they?' Most of the children remember the animals, and are able to say that there was an ox and a donkey. 'What was the donkey used for?' I'd ask, trying to get them to tell me that it brought Mary to Bethlehem.

Not the answer I was to get from one child. 'Donkey racing!' he announced. Looking up at the parent, I smiled. 'We, er, watched donkey racing when we went on holiday. I expect that is what he is remembering', laughed Dad apologetically.

I try to get the names of the children before they go in to the grotto, but so many names now are very different and I have a problem with remembering names anyway – so when I get there I usually have to resort to the excuse of saying 'I think you're old enough to tell Father Christmas your own name, aren't you?' and cross my fingers behind my back!

Derek actually does a super job as a representative of Father Christmas – who would be far too busy to meet all the children before Christmas, as he is busy making all the presents. Derek being Father Christmas all stems from my involvement many years ago at the local playgroup when our two youngest boys were attending. Somehow or other, and I can't remember why, I started to dress up for the summer fete: first as a clown, and then one year we were dressed in Victorian swimming costumes so that people could throw sponges at us. God, what we do to raise money! This silliness has helped me through a career in hotels and holiday camps in a previous life.

All very bizarre, as far as Derek is concerned, who was disgusted at my involvement in a sponsored bed-push to a local resort dressed in nightdress and curlers (I received no sympathy for the blisters or aching legs) and even more horrified when I dressed up as Donald Duck. Now this was a super costume which

. . . a lifesize Donald Duck sitting next to him!

involved a lovely white fluffy head complete with sailor's hat and orange beak. The baggy blue trousers and braces probably were not so impressive, but the *pièces de résistance* were the yellow tights and orange flippers. Unfortunately, in order to get the flippers to stay on, I needed to wear a pair of trainers.

The idea was to turn up at the playgroup and to tell the children that they could see me again at the fete. We therefore hoped that the children would nag their parents to come. Completely kitted up, I required a chauffeur to transport me to the village hall which, sadly for him, fell to Derek. His face mirrored his feelings on the matter but he dutifully agreed to do it. With us both seated in the car, we swung out on to the main road only to pass Derek's Uncle Den who was obviously most surprised to see Derek with a lifesize Donald Duck sitting next to him! 'It's alright for you,' Derek growled. 'No one can see who you are but I am quite obviously me.' I tried very hard but I am sure the fluffy head must have vibrated as I tried hard to restrain the tears of laughter during the silent journey to the playschool.

The biggest worry was that our children would recognise me, but no, all the children were thrilled at Donald Duck arriving from Disneyland, even though the walk with flippers was somewhat inexperienced. Only Simon's friend, Robert Fisher, was to notice the flaw. When I had said my spiel of 'come to the fete', he followed me out to the door and tugged at my tail which stuck out from the baggy blue trousers (quite a nice tail really, although it had been difficult to sit on in the car!), and confided to me as he bent his head next to mine and whispered, 'You're not the real Donald Duck – you've got trainers on.'

'Shhh!' I murmured, putting my white gloved finger to my beak. 'That will have to be our secret!' Giving him a thumbs-up, our bargain was struck and he ran happily back to the others.

I returned to my more than happy chauffeur (!) and went home. As a way of getting the Press to the fete, we arranged a photo call with 'Donald Duck' at the start of the fete. When the picture was duly taken I gratefully took the costume off as it was a very hot day, and changed into the Victorian costume for the water-throwing. Children have a wonderful way of being very unrelenting when throwing icy cold wet sponges at grown-ups held in wooden stocks, and all too often the sponges are on target and thrown quite hard, causing the desired effect of gasps and false faces of rage! Unfortunately, the wetter you are, the more children there seem to be queued up waiting for another go, and at times it is difficult to remember that it is all for a good cause!

I was therefore quite relieved (in a way) when an irate parent turned up with a crying child, and explained that the child was upset because she had missed seeing Donald Duck. The only reason this little girl had come was to see Donald Duck, whom she had seen at playschool, but who, it appeared, had now gone.

Towelling my hair dry, I assured the mother and child that as yet Donald Duck had not flown home, and if she waited a few minutes, I would try to find him. Chasing up the stairs, I quickly went to the bedroom where the costume was still laid out on the bed, and as quickly as possible tried to get dressed up. You can imagine the difficulty: peeling off my wet striped costume and attempting an element of speed, with the child's crying still to be heard on the front lawn, and me desperately pulling yellow tights up legs that were still wet.

Her mother having comforted her and with the thoughts of Donald Duck appearing, the small girl looked expectantly at the front door waiting for her 'hero'. And at last, head stuffed on and flippers going nineteen to the dozen, I mastered the stairs. With a grand entrance from the front door I held my arms out to her, expecting her to be pleased. She took one look at me, screamed and clung desperately to her mother, refusing to look. 'That's funny,' said her mother, walking away with her, 'she didn't like him at the playgroup either!'

With drooping head, I returned to the oh, so attractive wet swimming suit, to resume duties – why do I bother!

It was from this association that, when the original Father Christmas was unable to attend the playgroup Christmas party, Derek was thought to be the next best thing, and so it has become a custom. We do not have an age limit for going to see Father Christmas but do have a weight limit as to who can sit on his knee! Some of the requests are not always easy to promise. One small boy wanted a baby brother, to which Father Christmas said that he needed to talk to his Mum and Dad. Another young lady brought her daughter as her husband was 'again' playing rugby. 'I, Father Christmas, would like a new man!' she stated, as her daughter sat on Derek's knee.

'Well,' said Derek tactfully and looking at the young girl, 'perhaps Daddy will give up playing quite so much.'

'Oh, no,' said the lady, quite horrified, 'I wouldn't want him to do that – I just want a *new man!*' And from the look on her face she meant it!

With the finishing touches added to the decorations, I stood back to admire the effect. This room with the inglenook fireplace, affectionately known as the 'lazy room', will always be a room with many memories although our home is now upstairs on the first floor. The lazy room is the part of the tearoom that used to be the family room, and it would have the Christmas tree in it with all the presents underneath. After midday on Christmas Eve no one was allowed in it until Christmas morning. This was the room used to hide two goldfish in a bowl on one Christmas Eve. Our son Daniel, then aged seven, had bought them for his five-year-old brother, Simon. We had dutifully purchased them and secreted them in there ready for Christmas Day. To this day I have never known the proper name for them, but we had called them 'bobble-eyed' fish as they have huge bulbous eyes with fan tails and they were Simon's favourite.

Daniel was so excited at having got Simon a present he would really, really want, and when the next morning arrived he could not wait to run into the room to show Simon. Sadly, we had slipped up and not just the goldfish had been hidden in the room overnight. When they burst into the room on Christmas Day, the first thing that Daniel noticed was the cat sitting on the windowsill. 'Oh,' called out Daniel innocently, 'Blackie the cat is in here.' The second thing he noticed – was the empty bowl! As you can imagine, it was tears all round.

This sorrowful tale was to be rectified when my friend Sheena, who is also Simon's godmother, came down after Christmas and promised to take both Simon and Daniel out to purchase replacements. Sheena has never married or had children but is very good with children, although she does tend to indulge them – which will often result in her taking the kids out only to bring them back having eaten so much chocolate that they are feeling quite sick, and being a big child at heart herself, will often return in the same condition herself. So you can see why Sheena is always a popular visitor!

Sheena and I go back many years and have worked together in hotels as well as running a pub together. She has a terrific sense of humour but does like to get things right. She came back with both the boys in fits of laughter, most appalled that she had gone round to four or five pet shops asking for 'bobble-eyed fish' and had received some very odd looks. Only at the final shop had she been told the correct name for the fish she was looking for!

Henry

If dear old Henry was alive now, he too would have fond memories of the lazy room. Henry was a basset hound and if you have ever been an owner of one of these 'endearing dogs' you will have sympathy for any other person in a similar position! My sister June, who lives in Kent, had a basset for many years and when my parents visited they were very taken with him. They decided that when they were ready to have another dog, they would quite like to have one. When the time finally came, and despite the warning from June as to their obstinate streak (the basset – not my parents), a basset was found from the Basset Rescue Club.

Henry was about two years old, and from day one he made it quite clear that if he wanted to do what you wanted to do, that was fine, but if he wanted to do anything that you did not want him to do, he was going to do it anyway! He was a lovely dog though: coloured black, brown and white, he was a typical basset with the long stout body, very short legs with huge paws and the long drooping ears that scraped the ground. My parents live not very far from us and we were to hear of his escapades.

My parents struggled with him for over a year and then, being in their sixties, decided that such a strong-willed dog was not what they needed. One of the biggest problems was that he was very strong, and my mother being quite small, he would nearly pull her over when on the lead and would not always return if let off the lead. His daily walks were often longer than Dad would have wished as he stood calling to Henry to come back and have his lead put on. One day when I was at their flat, opposite the sea at Burnham, I joined Dad for a walk with Henry. It was winter and, wrapped up in warm clothes, Dad had his cap, raincoat and walking stick. Allowed off his lead, Henry nosed around and explored the sandy beach. To start with all went well, until Henry sighted an attractive labrador in the distance and despite my father's attempts at commands of return (a retired policeman, he is very good at commands) Henry was either deaf or indifferent.

Ears flying in the wind, Henry was on a mission. Finally having been chased into the distance, the labrador turned and was running back towards us with Henry hot on her heels. With my father frantically holding on to his hat in the wind and his coat flapping, he tried to assess the situation. It was obvious from his speed that Henry was not thinking of stopping when he passed us, so with quick thinking, Father turned his walking stick round so that he could hook the handle around Henry's neck as he passed, thus allowing Father to put Henry back on his lead. This motion was deftly carried out only to result in the dog flying up in mid air and turning a complete 180 degrees to continue running in the opposite direction, chasing nothing. For the sake of my parents' marriage, Henry came to live with us!

Henry was lovable in himself but was definitely a one-person dog and took a bit more notice of me than anyone else in the family – more by luck than for any qualities. He enjoyed life on the farm and got on very well with our red setter. He disliked intensely being left behind if we went out, and it was sometimes difficult to shut the door with him using all the power he had to try and prise it open and follow you.

. . . resulting in the dog flying up in mid air . . .

Once, we had just managed to get out and were in the car about to leave the yard, when I looked back at the house. 'Derek,' I said, 'we can't go.'

'What now?' he sighed, having just recovered from the battle of getting out.

'Henry is on the roof,' I said.

'What!' he said, frowning at me.

'Henry is on the roof,' I repeated.

We both got out of the car to see Henry barking as he stood on the roof ridge of the backhouse. On the final shutting of the back door, he had hurtled upstairs to where unfortunately a bedroom door had been left open. With sheer determination, he had cleared the window ledge, out on the roof, and was now quite proud of the fact that he had delayed our departure.

Anyone who has been in this position will know that you stand encouraging the dog to come down to you, and with tail wagging, they will come just within your reach – but as you go to pick them up, they pull back! This game proceeded for quite a long time and the 'Here, boy, good dog' was stated more and more between gritted teeth from Derek as he stood on a stepladder attempting to get him down. Of course I, as usual, was ever helpful, standing at the bottom in fits of laughter.

Eventually the day was won as we did get out and Henry was left behind (having made sure the bedroom doors were shut, this time), but we were very late!

Dog on the Roof

Dogs don't always have nice ideas of things that taste good, and one morning Derek came up for breakfast to inform me that Henry was sitting in the middle of the cow yard eating some afterbirth from one of the cows. He said he had told Henry 'don't eat that, you dirty dog', and had picked up a pitchfork and gone towards Henry expecting him to drop it, so that Derek could pick it up and throw it in with the manure. Not a bit of it. Henry squared up to Derek and indeed, sensing that his growling was disarming Derek, he walked towards Derek who decided to back off, and walking backwards was eventually evicted from the cattle yard.

'As far as I'm concerned' said Derek dissociating himself from the situation, 'if it makes him sick it will be his own fault.' Henry 1, Derek 0.

Henry was not sick and in fact, in some respects, his taste buds were very good. Kelly, our daughter, in her early teens, was very proud that she had made our Christmas cake and it really had turned out quite well. (Much to my relief, as the cost of the ingredients had been triple what it was to buy one!) Iced complete with snowman on top, she had brought it home and proudly presented it to us as soon as she returned from school. Leaving it on the kitchen table, she dashed off to do her homework and we, not thinking, went out to work on the farm. We were not the only people to be impressed by the Christmas cake: five minutes was all it took for Henry to reach the table top and to consume totally an 8-inch iced cake, leaving only the snowman.

After this event Kelly's affections towards Henry were on a similar basis to Derek's. I have this (no doubt very annoying) quality of being able to look on the bright side of things. 'Well, at least we shan't be without a Christmas cake, as there will be one in the hamper,' I said, 'although', I quickly soothed to a very upset Kelly, 'it obviously won't be as nice as your Christmas cake would have been!'

Not a bit of it – guess who got shut in the lazy room with the Christmas hamper when it arrived? And what was the only thing he ate totally out of all the assortment of goodies strewn around the room – the Christmas cake! And he still wasn't sick. But at Easter he was. Nobody rated him very highly when he managed to eat his way through six Easter eggs in one night. And he was so sick – he was a picture of dejection, with his ears sliding down either side of his head and his sad eyes and drooling, watering mouth – feeling very, very poorly indeed.

But apart from these annoying little habits (!) he was a super dog whom we all loved, and we were very sad when he was accidentally run over by a car in the yard, when the driver did not realise he was there. For all that Derek would moan about him, I think he was probably the most upset.

With Christmas decorations finished, it is time to concentrate on the wrapping of presents and writing of cards, and there is plenty of that. We try to acknowledge all the hard work that our staff and volunteers do throughout the year in helping us at all times of night or day, so there are a lot of people to remember.

Although much of the care work is carried out by our animal care assistants, volunteers come in mornings and evenings to help with the many wildlife casualties that are brought in to us. One of the first things that volunteers have to learn is that the last thing they must be is squeamish. Many animals will come in complete with maggots or fleas, and when it comes to feeding them, trying to give as natural a diet as possible will often result in having to de-head and squeeze out mealworms, and, more often than not, to cut up dead day-old chicks.

Terri and Heather, both mums with young children at school, would come in on a Tuesday morning. They didn't mind what they did, but Terri could not bring herself to deal with the dead chicks. She could not even pick one up, so she had managed to work a system with Heather that Terri would clean the cages and Heather could do 'that side of things', and we all teased her about her fear. Coming into the hospital room one morning, I found Terri busy chatting to Heather across the room. Terri was busy wiping the inside of a metal cage having taken the hedgehog out for the cage to be cleaned. Engrossed in what she was saying to Heather, Terri's hand was doing a continuous circling motion against the side of the cage.

That's funny, I thought to myself, because I could see yellow in amongst the white cloth which Terri was cleaning with. At the same time Heather and I came to the conclusion that, un-wittingly, Terri had picked up an uneaten dead chick put in as food for the hedgehog with her cleaning cloth and was busy 'spreading' it around the cage. I'm afraid we both exploded into laughter. This was followed by an almighty scream from Terri when she realised what she had done and a stampede of staff entering the room to find out what had caused the blood-curdling noise. Not a very good example for the sign on the door saying PLEASE KEEP THIS ROOM AS QUIET AS POSSIBLE.

We are usually far more caring with regards to volunteers, which is why, I hope, many stay with us year in and year out.

Why is it that, when there is so much to do, machines decide to break down? My two older daughters from a previous marriage visited during Christmas week to exchange Christmas presents. I decided to do a meal in the tearoom and both my parents came over as well. It is easier for us all to meet up before Christmas as Wendy's career spans several countries and she lives in Germany with her husband Norbert. Kerry is in the mounted police in Bristol, and Tim her partner is in the force too so they often have duties over the Christmas period.

We don't get the chance to get together very often so it was a lively evening with much talking to catch up on recent news. Nice at the end of it all to put everything into the dear little dishwasher and forget all about it – until the next morning that is! All the dishes were still dirty so we called in the electrician (to mend the dishwasher – not to wash the dishes!).

When Pete Lovell arrived in the late afternoon, we commented that there had not been any sign of anything being wrong. Pete, having looked inside, decided to pull the whole of the machine out to have a look.

'Oh, look,' he said, 'you've got lots of sunflower seeds and peanuts down there.'

'What!' I exclaimed, peering inside the empty space. It is always a shock when anyone decides to move such items in my kitchen as 'out of sight, out of mind' does tend to be my policy with regards housework – but even I was surprised at the seeds and nuts stored in amongst the fluff, bits of paper and the odd coin.

When Pete turned the dishwasher round and took the back of it off, he was to get another surprise. Almost all of the workings were compacted in peat, hay and sunflower seed cases, and right in the middle was the most beautiful nest of shredded paper and hay. And there peeping out with its little striped head was a blasted chipmunk that had obviously tunnelled from its aviary just outside the kitchen, through the stone wall and into the dishwasher, which doubtless had offered warm accommodation especially when on 'hot wash'.

'Oh, my goodness, it's a wonder the poor little thing hasn't been electrified,' said Pete. Derek's remark was more along the lines that maybe it would have been better if it had. But within the next few seconds, the chipmunk sprang from its cosy home and proceeded to bounce and somersault around the kitchen with plates on the dresser precariously rattling as all three of us attempted to capture the 'poor little thing'. Bright-eyed and bushy-tailed this one certainly was, and on finding the space the dishwasher had come out of, it practically gave us all a wave and disappeared back down the hole to its outside aviary.

Jamming the hole up, and checking that it had indeed returned to its aviary, it was clear that tomorrow's first job was to catch the chipmunks, partially dismantle the aviary and clad the wall. Derek took this all in good heart (joke). Late afternoon was becoming early evening and after a hard day outside, Derek's enthusiasm started to wane at the thought of having to mix up cement and block the hole through to the kitchen, clear up all the mess that Pete had cleared out of the back of the dishwasher (which was now working and Pete was gone), put the machine back under the work surface and get everything ship-shape.

These are the times when the comments 'you and your animals' and 'why did you want chipmunks anyway' trip easily from his tongue, when his chair and newspaper seem a long way away. Feeling that silence was probably the best tactic, I helped wash the floor and left him to put the dishwasher back under the work surface while I got tea.

'That's it!' Derek said as he sank back into the kitchen armchair with the newspaper after having his tea. 'Thank God that's over. Oh, by the way, I started the programme on the dishwasher to give it a clean.'

'Oh good, that's great' I said, surprised at his thoughtfulness. 'I'll check everything's OK when I go down to put the dogs out.'

Sadly, I was back in a few minutes. 'Er, the tide's in downstairs! Seems like there's rather a lot of water on the floor in the kitchen!' I murmured. Derek had forgotten to put the outlet pipe back in the drain as he put the machine back in – he did not read much of his paper that evening!

Quite a few of the staff look forward to my father's Rum Pot which he makes throughout the year. It is a potent creation of all the summer fruits layered with rum and allowed to soak. By Christmas, it is a dessert to eat when you aren't going out anywhere but, by George, it warms you up! My father does Reception for us at our Centre on certain days and rules the staff with a rod of iron when it comes to collecting the syndicate lottery money. He collects the clotted cream from the local farm for our delicious cream teas and is an absolute gem for doing all my ironing.

Dad is very good, doing a great deal of running about for his sister Lillian, now in her eighties and living in the town of Clevedon which is about half an hour from us. Aunt Lillian finds it difficult to move around these days but keeps wonderfully cheerful and still enjoys life. A few years ago, my father came back from Clevedon having visited not only Aunt Lillian but also Auntie Rose, who was living in a sheltered home and has since sadly died. She had lost most of her sight and was also partially deaf.

He was amused to tell us that, when he arrived at Auntie Rose's flat, she had complained that her hearing aid was not working so she had put it in the drawer by the bed. Checking for her, Dad found the object and handed it to her saying, 'Is this what you mean?'

Turning it in her hand, Auntie Rose said, 'Yes, but it's not working I tell you.' She handed it back to Dad.

'This,' said Dad, trying to get her to hear, 'is a piece of crystallized ginger that I gave to you before I left last time!'

'So,' my father said to me, shaking his head, 'if you go over to see Auntie Rose and she's got a piece of crystallized ginger in her ear – you'll know why!'

I don't want to get old!

Christmas Day and Boxing Day usually pass very quickly as, although a few of our staff turn out, we try to help in the mornings and do all the afternoon feeds ourselves, so after Christmas lunch it is back outside to work. But it is still a lovely time catching up with all the family. We usually see Kelly with her husband Richard, now with their own family of three small boys, as they live in nearby Bridgwater, and our older sons, Daniel in London and Barry in Brighton, usually come home for at least a day or two. Simon with his girlfriend Nikki managed to ring us from Australia where they were travelling around for a year, and it seemed odd to hear that they were basking in the sun

17

by the pool. They are both quite interested in animals and it was lovely to hear about the beautiful variety of birds and animals they had been lucky enough to see.

I was hoping they would have the chance to visit a friend of mine who lives in Australia and does rehabilitation work like me, but for wombats rather than badgers, which is my main interest. When Manuela last wrote she sent some pictures of her orphan 'babes'. People think I must be mad to work with badgers as they are very strong animals that have a strong bite, due to their territorial nature, but in fact they are quite easy to handle despite the possibility of an adult weighing up to 15 to 18 kilos. But Manuela is working with animals that have huge claws and the ability to reach 40 kilos in weight: a 'lot of bulldozer', as she puts it in her letters! She also does snake rescues, and most of the snakes in Australia are highly venomous – puts our rescues of the odd grass snake to shame! I applaud her efforts.

You can only work with wildlife in Australia under licence with the National Parks and Wildlife Service. It is necessary to have attended a course in respect of the species you are dealing with. They also have vets who will work with wildlife and will not charge for their time, only for the drugs and equipment used. Despite our reputation as a nation of animal lovers, vets prepared to help with wildlife are far and few between. One of the main failings is that within their six-year university life they will only receive approximately 15 hours of tuition on British wildlife, if they are lucky.

There is no legislation that protects our wildlife when taken into care for welfare reasons. No standards of care, no ethics that have to be abided by. It is up to each individual to decide on quality of life and standard of accommodation. As every person differs in their views, so also are the lives of animals dependent on their carers' criteria.

The many programmes on television certainly promote the need to care for wildlife, but in reality it is still often thought that wildlife feel no pain and therefore simple first aid, pain killers and treatment are all too often denied them. It is frustrating, to say the least, to have animals brought into us *after* they have been to a vet with such things as broken backs, dislocated hips and compound fractures which mean that the animal certainly should not have been transported in such a condition had it been examined properly.

18

It is wrong to make a sweeping statement about vets in general when there are many who will go to extraordinary lengths to help wildlife, but the fact that such things happen means that we are a long way from the caring reputation that the media say we have. All too often pain and suffering is caused by people with the best will in the world, who believe they are being kind, through ignorance of the species they are dealing with. We desperately need a means of controlling the capture, care and release of our wildlife through legislation that is put into place for their protection.

For us, Boxing Day is usually the day for going for a walk and it is a day when you can almost guarantee a call-out to an injured animal. This year it was a late afternoon call to a seabird. A young couple spending a few days down in some holiday cottages in Brean had gone for a stroll along the beach. They had noticed a seabird unable to fly and when it did not attempt to move when they tried to catch it, they took it back home to warm it up. At a loss to know what to do next, they gave us a ring. By the time I arrived with cage in hand it was already quite dark, but I was able to find their cottage quite easily. They had quite rightly supported the bird with a towel and placed it in a box.

It was a guillemot and as there appeared to be no apparent injuries or abnormalities other than being incredibly light, I assumed that it was exhausted and starving due to the recent storms. In its winter plumage it was not so impressive as when the dark brown colouring covers the upper parts of its body, making it look very sleek. They spend most of their time at sea except when nesting on the cliffs during their breeding season (from March to July), and they have quite a long and sharp beak – something to be aware of – but not this one, who was too weak to put up a fight.

Pleased that the bird was going somewhere to be looked after, the couple bade me farewell and it was not long before I was installing it in our hospital room under a warm heat lamp with fish defrosting in a nearby bowl ready to feed him when he improved. Once we have stabilized a bird, we will usually pass it on to our nearby RSPCA wildlife unit at West Hatch, near Taunton, as they are very experienced with seabirds. But for now, watching him under the red glow of the heat lamp, he is safe and warm. The room's long white units and centre island are mainly empty. Heat lamps all in rows hang idle, waiting for the time when the room will be filled with orphaned and injured animals that flood the centre once spring arrives. Glancing around the hospital room as I turn the light out, I can just see in the red light that the guillemot has settled and the few residents, mainly hedgehogs, are quietly snoozing.

In a few days a new year will start and we await the next season, which undoubtedly will bring a huge variety of animals in to us.

2

Bubble Gum Deer

I started the New Year with mixed feelings towards carrying on my wildlife work. Only the previous year, in September, my special badger called Bluebell had died. She had been with us for nearly six years. I had a special affinity with her and, in a way, it was through her that my real dedication to wildlife started. With the ever-growing costs of caring for orphaned and injured animals, a charity was formed to help finance our work; it was named the Bluebell Sett after Blue, by then a very well-known badger.

We had an observation sett built on our farm for Bluebell and her siblings, who came to us as orphaned cubs, so that when they grew up they would have the chance of freedom. Bluebell was the only one who stayed and lived around the farm, and when she died, I could have quite easily given everything up. I hoped that the highs and lows of the future year would help me through. Little did I know that with so many lows in that year, I was going to wish I'd slept through it completely!

In late October, as the sett was empty, we were asked by the RSPCA to look after two badgers that had been reared by people who had allowed them to become too tame. Despite being passed on to the RSPCA they had not as yet reverted to being wild, and as they were male, the RSPCA would, quite correctly, not think of releasing them. No wild animal should be released with a trust in human beings, as sadly this is often abused; and if an animal is what we called 'imprinted' there are other dangers too.

'Imprinted' means that the animal fails to understand what species it belongs to and associates itself with humans, as during its upbringing it has only been fed by humans and not allowed to interact with its own kind. The problem with this is that often the animal will still develop natural instincts but these will be used in incorrect ways. Badgers, especially male ones, as they get older develop their territorial nature and will protect their own 'area'. This can lead to problems, particularly with people involved in caring for badgers.

For example, badger expert Phil Drabble reared a male badger cub who dug his own sett in Phil's garden when given his freedom. Through the years he would routinely visit the house to see Phil every night. Whilst in the house (Phil's territory) the male would remain friendly but once the badger went outside, if Phil went out into the garden, the male badger would chase him back indoors as he was not prepared to share his territory with him. This is a natural thing for a badger to do, to chase 'other badgers' away if they are not wanted in their area. Therefore a confused animal can prove dangerous.

The two badgers, one named Morgan and the other Paddy, came to us in late autumn in the hope that, taken away from their original carer and placed in a new environment, they would revert to being wild. As soon as the badgers went into the observation sett and enclosure they showed no interest in me, and after putting food in the enclosure just before dark, we ceased all human contact. The only time I came anywhere near to the badgers was when it was necessary to clean the glass in the front of their chambers. Again they were not able to get near me and as they turned wild, I would hope that the very fact of my being present would initiate a desire to run away and hide.

With Paddy this was not very noticeable and as time went on, he would stay in the chamber and growl. Eventually, as he got older, Paddy would actually throw himself at the glass in an attempt to get at me. Sadly, I got the same reaction in the enclosure and it necessitated a very quick exit. I needed help with this situation. All my work with the RSPCA is done in connection with Colin Seddon who has been at the Wildlife Unit in Taunton for many years, and I can count on his support and advice that has come from dealing with badgers for many, many years. With heavy heart, I contacted Colin, knowing that if he agreed with my thoughts it was very probable that we would end up euthanasing this badger. It is rarely acceptable to keep a wild animal in captivity, but one that can injure staff is irresponsible too, no matter how much you care.

When Colin arrived we both went down to the sett and watched the badgers in the chambers. They were both fine adult males by now, in really good condition and looking well.

'I really hope I'm wrong', I said to Colin.

'Well, if you aren't, it's not going to be your fault. It was their second chance to come here, so let's see', Colin answered.

Unlocking the door, it was Colin who went in by the chambers to see if the hate was just aimed at me. Immediately sensing the close contact, Morgan shot out of the chamber into the tunnels behind but Paddy literally threw himself at the glass, working hard with his claws to try and get out. Even Colin was shocked at the vehemence of Paddy's reactions.

Checking him also in the alleyway and obtaining the same response, Colin's interpretation of his behaviour was the same as mine. 'He is a dangerous animal,' Colin said, 'and the sooner we put him down for your safety, the happier I shall be. We need to arrange for a vet to come out and I will come and help you catch him.'

At this time the BBC were starting to work with the RSPCA on a series of programmes due to be broadcast in 1996 called 'Back to the Wild'. It was a kind of fly-on-the-wall programme, so hearing what was happening, they wanted to come and film the proceedings. It seemed rather macabre on first thoughts, but Colin and I then decided that perhaps it would bring home the fact that caring for all wildlife has to be done in the correct way, otherwise these things will happen.

The day they came I found it very difficult to cope with. I still found the loss of Bluebell very distressing and the thought of having to put down a healthy, albeit dangerous, animal, and at my instigation, was very hard.

Catching was done very quickly and easily and the whole procedure was carried out without any stress or suffering, first anaesthetising the badger in a crush cage and then euthanasing it. The film crew, give them their due, followed it all without causing any disruption or prolonging of the event. It was at the final administering of the euthanasia that I could no longer hold in my feelings and I turned and walked away.

The producer, realising what was happening, signalled the camera to follow and I found myself being interviewed whilst in floods of tears. Did it really bring home the heartache of failure, the waste of a life, the little bit of you that dies when you know that you have caused an animal to be killed? I don't know, but to this day, I still say that if you can take putting an animal down lightly – it's time you stopped doing it.

At least one animal survived: Morgan was released, leaving our sett empty for the family of cubs due to arrive.

It is not just badgers that get confused by imprinting. Even our barn owl, Sage, who has been with us for many years, will swoop down and sink his talons into a dog if he gets the chance. Not that he's thinking of having one for dinner, he just doesn't like them, but his mind is confused into believing he is a human as he was hand-reared by a young man from day one of hatching. His natural instinct of catching with his talons is confused with his dislike of dogs – but he will happily sit on your shoulder and preen through your hair!

Dot

Another typical example is Dot the red deer who came to us as a juvenile, having been hand-reared on the bottle by the lady who found her. She did a super job, but sadly Dot was never put with her own kind and therefore considered herself human. She came to us and was so tame that she would follow us around everywhere.

Despite being very friendly, we could not understand why occasionally she would rear up on her hind legs and really go at you quite hard with her front feet. Her hooves being very sharp, this could be quite dangerous, particularly with children. We then realised that, coming to a new home, all she wanted to know was where she stood in the pecking order of this new 'herd' that she had joined. Mandy, our animal supervisor, and myself would pull her feet down and thus earned respect from her – Derek too, who would manhandle her, never a man to be bettered by an animal (except Henry!). The other girls, because they were a bit afraid of her, were well down on her list and if it was their turn to put her away at night she would soon stand her ground if she was in no hurry to go in, and dare them to do anything about it!

Dot was lovely to have around even though the flowers took a bit of a hammering. To see her skitting around was super. However, once spring arrived and doors needed to be left open, it was hard to explain to her that visitors in the tearoom did not want a deer chewing their ear while they are having a cream tea, and poor John, who worked in Reception, got so cross when Dot would come in and tip things over.

John came to us when he retired, and to start with used to take admission money in a small kiosk by the entrance where he could listen to cricket on his radio and read the paper when he wasn't busy. Progress being what it is, we now have a new entrance with a Reception and he now takes the admission money . . . and answers the telephone . . . and sells the sweets from the shop area . . . and the added annoyance of a red deer who came in and made a bee-line for the rainbow bubble gum was almost more that he could stand.

'Look at this! Look at this!' John said to me as I evicted Dot once more from the shop area of Reception, waving a plastic tube of bubble gum. Walking back I looked at what he was waving in his hand. She had knocked the whole box over and had been sucking quite hard on this packet; the first yellow ball was quite wet with saliva even though it was still in the packet. The saliva had dribbled down past the next two balls of bubble gum but the rest looked quite dry.

'What am I meant to do with this then!' he raged.

'Well,' I mused, looking at the sweets, 'I personally probably wouldn't eat the first few but the rest should be OK if you want to have them.'

'I don't want to eat them!' he spluttered. 'You've got to do something about her – she's in here every morning!'

Retreating, I had to admit he was right. It was time to put her in a pen. We tried her with sheep and with goats but she really did not like any of it and just wanted to be out. Discussing the problem with Colin, he came up with the suggestion of contacting a lady called Mary-Lee who kept red and fallow deer and often liked tame ones to help her move them from paddock to paddock. We telephoned Mary-Lee and she agreed to take her. The next problem was how to move Dot as deer are incredibly nervous and they can easily break legs if they panic during transportation. It was finally arranged that Liz our vet would help anaesthetise her and travel with us, keeping her sedated until she arrived at her new home. We were all very worried for we knew it could all go seriously wrong and, loving Dot as we did, we certainly did not want to hurt her in any way.

The day arrived and Liz turned up with her black box of goodies. She is in her thirties, small and slim with long black hair she can hide behind if she feels like it! Her association with us has certainly broadened her spectrum of life, which was about to be made even broader with a journey in the back of the van with a deer.

The plan was to take Dot her morning feed and quickly inject her before she realised anything was up. Well of course, for no apparent reason Dot decided she was not going to behave routinely. Running up for her feed as usual, she came within a couple of feet of me, sensed that something was afoot and bounded off into the distant corner of her pen where she turned and watched in anticipation.

There was absolutely no point in trying any other ploys, and joining Derek and Liz who had been hiding behind the outbuilding, we decided to go for a coffee and rethink the situation. The journey was going to take two hours and we were keen not to be travelling in the heat of midday. The problem was to get Dot in a position where we could hold her while Liz injected her and it would probably need Derek's strength as well as my own to do this. But any sign of Derek when I went out there would soon ring warning bells as it was completely different from her usual routine.

Derek drove the van out to near the pen but remained inside ready for the second attempt. With ears pricked up, Dot took this all in but as no one got out of the van she discarded the activity as a threat. Liz and I then, casually talking, walked out to the pen and Dot bounded over to us, her desire for food overcoming her sense of caution.

Walking her round the gate and beside the van, Derek quickly opened the door forcing Dot against the gate of the fence. It was just enough time for Liz to slip the needle in and to move the van door before fear made Dot carry out any movements, such as jumping, that could injure her limbs. Standing facing us now, she snorted with indignation and lifted her upper lip to show that she disapproved of whatever we had just done, although she wasn't sure what it was. Stamping her feet, Dot moved away, but already she was losing co-ordination of her legs and we stood aside to allow her to settle as she became sleepy and finally unconscious.

We moved quickly. The van had been lined with straw bales and blankets to protect her. We knew that if things went wrong and she thrashed out and broke her legs, we could easily end up putting her down. I was reminded of the worrying journey when Dot first came to us, and here we were, putting her at risk again. I so hoped that we were doing the right thing for her. Placing Dot in an upright position in the back of the van, Liz sat alongside her with stethoscope handy to monitor her breathing as we travelled along. We were soon on our way.

The first part of the journey was on the motorway and all went well; we pulled off at Exeter and were on country roads the rest of the way. Occasionally I looked over at Liz checking Dot.

'Is she alright?' I asked.

'She's fine', said Liz; 'Her breathing is regular.'

I couldn't help repeating the question at different times, I was so worried that everything was going to go smoothly. However, the next time I asked, I felt that Liz was concerned. She seemed to be slightly worried and when I looked again, she was definitely looking paler.

'Are you sure Dot's alright?' I asked anxiously. I was sure that something was not quite right and Liz was holding out on me. 'You really look quite worried – are we losing her?'

'She', said Liz, 'is perfectly fine but', she said, wiping a weary hand over her face, 'if you don't stop this van and let me get out to be sick there'll be a terrible mess in here!'

My constant caring thoughts had been for Dot and I had not realised that, sitting in the back of the van, Liz had been feeling more and more sick as time and the winding road went on. And sick she was – most unbecoming for a vet! The rest of the journey, I was in the back and Liz was in the front.

Dot was still very sleepy when we arrived. As we had driven deeper and deeper into Devon, through the valleys and wooded landscape, it had become obvious what a beautiful part of the country Dot was coming to. Mary-Lee's house was perfect. Built on the side of a hill, she could see for miles and in her lounge she has a huge telescope so that she could watch her herds, wherever they were on her land.

Mary-Lee greeted us on arrival and we immediately unloaded Dot into a corner of a barn deep with fresh straw. We waited with her as she slowly came round and seemed totally unfazed by her new surroundings. We stayed for a while and Mary-Lee promised to let us know how she got on. All too soon it was time to leave Dot behind in her new home. Needless to say, Liz again travelled in the front!

It took a long time for Dot to accept that the long-legged animals she shared a field with were deer the same as her, and she still spent a great deal of time with Mary-Lee as she worked around her farm.

Two years later, Colin was to report that Dot had a calf at foot so someone must have taught her that she was a deer after all!

As January is a quiet time of year for most people, our local badger group had arranged with the police to have a training day for police officers to make them more conversant with the Badger Act. In the morning there was to be a talk on badgers, explaining their lifestyle and the kind of problems that occur, and in the afternoon some of the group were to mock a badger dig in a nearby wood and the police were to follow a report and role-play the incident. This was to be followed by interviewing techniques back at the Training Centre.

There were approximately fifteen officers present on the day, which was very refreshing as many of these officers were wildlife liaison officers, often having to do this kind of course work in their own time. It is only their dedication to wildlife that promotes them to spend time trying to understand the sometimes very complicated and confusing legislation that covers all manner of offences.

The first hour was spent with a slide presentation about badgers, explaining the tracks and signs which would be put into practice during the afternoon session. Statistics were given as to the numbers still persecuted through digging and baiting, and this was followed by a very short video obtained from Court evidence showing badger digging. Even these adult men and women used to dealing with the worst side of human nature found it difficult to watch.

The film shows the 'fun' that diggers get having first attached radio-tracking collars to Jack Russell dogs and sending them down the sett to find the badger. The Jack Russell is not sent down to fight with the badger, just to find the badger and hold it at bay. Each time the badger turns to try and dig away, the terrier will nip the badger's rump to make it turn thus allowing the diggers above to locate the radio signal and know where to start digging to reach the animal.

Once the badger is reached, it is usually thrown to larger dogs, often two or three at a time. The sound of the dogs attacking the badgers, the goading of the dogs to continue fighting despite the injuries of ripped throats and deep wounds from a badger's powerful jaws, the filming of the badger being stabbed and shot and yet still desperately trying to reach freedom, was more than some of the officers could take and a few left the room.

Most badger digging is done by men from certain areas. It is a tradition that is often carried from father to son, although some women do get involved. The difference between digging and baiting was explained. For baiting the badger is taken away to another location. Experience helps these men know how to handle the badger: usually they are shy, retiring creatures, but if cornered a badger will use every ounce of strength to try and get free. Put in sack bags or metal crates these animals are taken to towns in a quiet location where a pit will be dug and metal-lined so the badger cannot get out. Often the badger will have its jaw or front leg broken to put it at a disadvantage before the fight begins.

Bets can reach thousands of pounds as different dogs are pitted against the badger, sometimes for a period of over three hours before the badger will finally find peace in death. As you can imagine, by the end of the morning session, we had some very enthusiastic police officers who would act very quickly in the future if informed of a possible dig. A maximum fine of £3,000 and a custodial sentence of up to three years may seem good preventative methods, but actually to obtain a prosecution is very difficult indeed.

This was the point of having the role-play in the afternoon. Adrian Coward, who is the chairman of the Somerset Trust Badger Group, myself and two other members were to be involved.

Given a woodland grid reference we were at the scene by 2.30. With a desperate lack of ownership of dogs, I had taken along our dog Barney, who is a labrador cross bearded collie. A more lovable, teddy bear type of dog you could not find – but, we decided, he was better than nothing.

We had a dead fox and a dead badger with us in bags, ones that had been killed on the road and that we had kept in the deep freeze for this event. Diggers will usually have a dead fox with them, as they will say they are digging for foxes, if discovered, as this is quite legal – so you can already see the difficulty in obtaining a prosecution. We had not got the animals out of the freezer soon enough because they were still slightly stiff – well, you can't get everything right can you?

The digging was to be in the vicinity of a sett: obviously we could not (it would be illegal) nor did we want to dig an actual sett, but we needed to be near one for tracks and signs. Adrian, Bryson and Alan were dressed in old clothes trying to look the part. We had spades, a hollow pipe (used to listen underground) and sack bags with us. I for my part was trying to get the dog interested in the digging and, of course, this hugely ferocious dog was more inclined to sit with tail wagging, bemused at all this unusual activity.

The motley crew were beginning to get quite tired of digging and were beginning to worry that we weren't going to be found, when the sudden crackling of branches and leaves heralded the onslaught of eight officers shouting at us that they were the police and we were to stand still. Adrian quickly slung the bag with the badger in it into the hedge.

Remember that they had no idea what was going to be there, or what we were going to say. They had just responded to a report of people seen in a wood acting strangely! The officers were quickly told that Adrian and his mate were merely digging for foxes. They already had one in a bag over there; 'No harm in that, mate', said Adrian, getting into character. Barney ran to greet the officers and lick their hands – turncoat!

We presented our story: the three men were digging for foxes, I was out walking my dog. They had approached me because they had lost their terrier down the hole and wanted me to see if my dog could scent where he was and bark to encourage him to come out. Amid all the confusion, Adrian kept angrily asking what was going to happen about his dog still down the hole (this was obviously untrue) and I was wailing that I had to go and fetch the children from school and if they kept me any longer, I would miss them and I was worried what was going to happen etc., etc.

We were asked to move away from the site and the officers were about to take our details. One officer reported to the sergeant that he had found the fox indicated, but as far as he was concerned it appeared not to be freshly killed and he considered it had been brought to the scene. When gravely asked how he had come to this conclusion, the young officer replied that it was mainly due to the icicles on its ears!

Another officer was getting very close to where the badger in the bag had been thrown, and no one was watching me so I decided to make a run for it through the wood. The first person to notice my exit was Barney, who was enthralled at joining me as we ran through the trees, but very quickly two more officers were in pursuit. Through the wood and halfway down the field, I have to say that I was beginning to feel I was winning until the sight of four uniformed officers coming up from the road direction proved that radio contact was of great benefit in these situations.

. . . mainly due to the icicles on its ears!

I was marched back to the site.

'What was that all about?' the panting officer sternly inquired.

'I wanted to get back and pick the kids up', I lied, leaning over and holding my knees, desperately trying to catch my breath.

Barney barked and pranced – that was good, looking sideways, he was ready to go again – I definitely wasn't !

In my absence they had found the dead badger and were all deciding what they could do within the law. Several of the officers had recognised tracks and signs to show that we were near a badger sett and realised the need to call an expert witness to verify their findings. In the Badger Act, there is no power of arrest. This is one of the biggest problems, as even if the police go back to the station and try to obtain a warrant to search the home premises of the people who are involved, by the time the police get there, any evidence that would incriminate these people will usually have been removed. However, you can confiscate any evidence from the scene, including vehicles and dogs, if you suspect a crime has been committed. In fact just recently, suspected diggers were held by the police deciding to confiscate their clothes and giving them the option to stay behind naked or return to the police station to remove their clothes!

Probably because of me being a nuisance, they decided to confiscate Barney. I argued over it but was sent away after being told to report to the police station at a later time to see if I would be allowed to have him back. I made them promise they would look after him.

Walking back down from the field, away from the officers, there was a peal of laughter as Barney, with no regard for the law, slipped his collar and hurtled down to catch me up.

Back at the training college, there was plenty of discussion as to other ways that the situation could have been handled and two of us went on to be interrogated in a mock interview room. The other officers were able to watch the whole role-play by camera link-up and it was videotaped.

Again, probably because of the trouble I had caused, I was chosen as one of the criminals. It is amazing how guilty you can feel in that kind of situation even when you know it is all pretence. Watching the video after and listening to the police officers discussing the methods of interviewing, you become aware of the body language that is used and the techniques of leaning towards you to intimidate you, and of the use of one officer as 'friend' and one as 'accuser'. A very interesting day for all.

Hopefully after the day, there were several police officers feeling far more confident if given a similar situation in real life. There was also a tired dog that had enjoyed a day in the woods with all those funny people, and on my part, two very aching legs!

Watching the news on television the next week, little did I realise the dramatic effect that one event was going to have on the lives of thousands of birds and all sea life in that area. A ship called the *Sea Empress* was reported as being grounded on some rocks at Milford Haven and there were worries about the spillage of oil during the night, as due to the storms expected that night, there was nothing that could be done until the next morning.

One of the worst incidents of oil pollution was to unfold the next day when thousands and thousands of gallons of oil spewed out into the sea as the ship was towed away from the rocks. It was acclaimed an unheralded pollution disaster which would affect the balance of nature to sea life for years and years to come. Pictures filled our screens of birds, seals and the whole coastal environment suffering as the thick black oil coating the waves took its toll.

Although it is at these times that wildlife rescue centres pull together and achieve incredible results, never will they be able to balance the damage that man, often unwittingly but sometimes intentionally, causes to our environment. Whilst the RSPCA leads in these situations, it is often through the manpower, charity and facilities of many, many people that the suffering is reduced as best we can.

Transportation of birds, holding points and washing facilities across the country were swamped by the sheer number of affected individuals. The RSPCA wildlife unit near us at Taunton alone was to deal with 1,500 birds, mainly scoters, guillemots and gulls but also diving birds. And where the oil found its way into the harbour, several swans were also affected.

Common scoters are usually known as sea ducks as they spend most of the winter out at sea, but they will also be found in freshwater lakes for breeding, mainly in Scotland and Ireland. They are quite a dark colour with the males being almost totally black with a black and yellow/orange bill and the female being a lighter greyish colour with pale cheeks. When out at sea in the winter, especially in stormy weather, they will float on the water together, closely packed, forming rafts. For this reason, they were the predominant species that suffered during this oil disaster.

Being a bird that spends most of its life on the water, one of the main problems with the scoters was that if they were in poor body condition, the breast would be thin and in captivity continual resting on the keel bone often caused injury.

Freezers were donated to house the large supplies of fish required to feed the birds, heat lamps were needed to keep the birds warm and a never-ending supply of washing-up liquid was required to wash the birds. Even the more fundamental items of towels and blankets which were desperately needed were handed in by people wishing to help in this huge rescue. There was simply no time to wash anything, and when soiled with oil, towels and blankets were often too difficult to clean anyway. Portacabins were hired, when all the holding space was taken up, to be able to take still more and more oiled birds as they arrived.

We sent staff down from Secret World, over a six-week period, to help out. When I went down, it was obvious from the exhausted faces the number of hours that these dedicated staff were putting in to try and treat as many birds as possible. West Hatch was rebuilt only recently but gone was the smart, tidy entrance. With the portacabins parked as close as possible to the building, electric leads snaked their way across the tarmac road. Wheelie bins were stacked together, ready to take the huge amount of waste that was coming out daily from all the cleaning. Newspapers stacked in piles by the front door were evidence of yet another delivery from well-wishers trying to help, as were the mountains of blankets and towels stacked in the Reception.

Sacks of mail, donations, offers of help, letters of disgust that such a disaster had happened as well as letters telling them they were wasting their time – all sat waiting to be opened and answered. The office staff were not only swamped by mail, but constant telephone calls blocked the switchboard – media wanting to know what was happening, volunteers ringing in to see if they could help, and some people, unable to comprehend the work going on 24 hours a day, ringing just to see 'how everything was going along'! The distinct smell of fish invaded every room, heightened by the warmth necessary for the birds who were no longer able to naturally keep their body temperature high enough due to loss of feather condition.

Every corner was taken up, either with cages needing to be cleaned, or containers of detergent. Wellingtons, coats and carriers were everywhere. Men and women of all ages wearing green overalls worked tirelessly: some with mops and buckets just trying desperately to keep everything clean, vets endeavouring to keep on top of the routine and monitoring the birds' progress. One lady spent her whole day, every day, defrosting fish and counting them out into containers according to size for each different species of bird. Management were trying to keep volunteers with things to do that were within their capabilities and qualified staff doggedly continued to carry out their duties which must, at many times, have appeared a never-ending situation.

The biggest problem in all these situations is the need for experienced staff, people who know how to handle the birds, people who recognise animals that are stressed and failing. There just wasn't the time even to show volunteers what to do, but having said that, there were many who turned up and were prepared to do anything, no matter how mundane – they were so useful, just to free the experienced staff, enabling them to do other jobs. And these people, the ones who just washed floors and cages and filled tubs with salt water and fish, were as important to the whole process as the ones washing and cleaning the birds.

Each single bird had a log number with a record sheet detailing breed, age, condition, treatment received so far. You can appreciate the credit due in such situations that made the whole strategy possible, no need to ask more from staff – they all worked together with a common interest for the animals they were dealing with.

Due to the numbers, a certain amount of assessment is vital in disaster situations as it is impossible to deal with all of the birds. On arrival some may be in too poor a body condition or, having ingested too much oil, are beyond help, in which case they are euthanased. There is just not the time to give to these birds, especially as experience has shown that they will not survive even if given the attention.

Every bird with a chance of survival is gavaged with rehydration fluids and charcoal. This means that a plastic tube is slipped down the throat into the stomach and a measured dosage given. This is where experienced handlers need to be involved, to hold the bird correctly and confidently and for the second person to make sure that the tube goes to the stomach and not to the lungs, which would kill the bird. Done expertly and quickly it causes little stress as the birds are used to consuming quite large items of food and a plastic tube slides down quite easily.

Any excess oil is wiped from their beaks and their feet and then they are allowed to rest in groups according to species. The rooms are divided into different sections. Of course, eventually there were so many birds that every single cage, every single nook and cranny was being used to accommodate them. Some rooms literally were filled floor to ceiling with cages, each containing a bird with the record sheet held on the front by a peg. The rooms are kept quiet and warm to help them get over the stress of captivity, transportation and gavaging.

As soon as possible, once in a stable condition, these birds need to be washed. This depends on the availability of carers to wash them and sinks being available. It takes two people to wash a bird, one to hold (that's the one who gets bitten and scratched – especially where scoters are concerned) and one to wash. A piece of rubber tubing is placed on the beak to stop the bird from biting, and with the bird's body being firmly held, the person washing starts with the head from the beak, down the neck to the shoulders, with constant application of washing-up liquid, warm water and a spray. Every inch is covered, from the neck down to the tail, to each wing in turn before turning the bird over and doing the complete underside of the wings and then the body.

It takes a full ten minutes for an experienced person to wash an oiled bird, not a job to be taken on by the inexperienced or in the wrong conditions. Each person is covered by a long rubber apron (but you still get very wet!), the room is exceptionally warm so as not to chill the birds and constant fresh warm water needs to be on hand to continually flush the bird with water. All the time the bird must be monitored and if it shows any sign of going into shock the washing must be stopped and the bird allowed to recover in a quiet area, or you will end up with a clean, dead bird which is no good to anyone.

Evidently there is now a new machine that can clean oiled birds. The birds are placed inside with their heads poking out and they go through a programme of cleaning. The fact that the head is not cleaned, which is the very first thing that needs to be done, will not reduce the handling of the bird and a machine is unlikely to notice if a bird is going into shock – it will still run the whole programme. I suppose the thinking is that the increase in numbers done in a set time compensates for the odd few that die in the machine. Why does progress result in money and time saving but less care for the individual concerned? So far, one of these machines has not been used at the wildlife unit at West Hatch and I don't think many staff are keen to use it.

After the first wash, the birds are placed back in warm rooms where preening will help get their feathers back into condition. One of the biggest problems was knowing the substance that was on the birds, as there are many kinds of oil each with different qualities. Many of the birds that were picked up over the three weeks after the disaster were affected by the dispersant agent that was being used on the oil; this leads to severe problems with the feathers not waterproofing after being cleaned, so there were many complex problems that the vets had to deal with at the Centre.

Usually the bird would have a second wash two or three days later, but sometimes up to a week later if lack of manpower made it impossible to do it sooner. After the second wash, if the bird was felt to be thoroughly clean, it would be put in a warm room overnight to preen and put its feathers in order before being placed outside in the pools in the enclosures. Once in condition, their feathers would be all these birds would need to keep themselves warm outside, even in winter. Used to the harsh storms on winter seas, an enclosure in Somerset must have been a doddle.

One of the problems that prevented birds being able to move on to the outside was how few pools were available at the RSPCA Centre. Usually only ten birds would be put in each pool (and they only had seven) and they would need to be in these pools for a week to regain condition before being released. Since this disaster, West Hatch have now obtained portable pools and therefore are now better equipped to cope with this kind of influx of birds.

Of course the other worry was that, when released from coastal regions, some birds might return to their original flight path and could again find themselves in the polluted areas. With all the human help in the world, nature cannot be changed.

Many television crews came to film the work being carried out and, while I was there, a short middle-aged lady called Jane Lacey came from BBC Radio. I was washing birds with Paul Kennedy. Paul's young studious face means that he is very often taken to be in his teens rather than in his late twenties. A very dedicated wildlife assistant, he does not always take too kindly to the interruption of the media and despairs of their limited knowledge.

I was holding the bird and Paul was preparing to start to soap and wash the bird. We were both attired in wellies and rubber aprons (over other clothes of course!), standing on wooden slates as the floor was wet and slippery. Standing at one side of the stainless steel sink, Paul was checking that the water from the spray nozzle was the right temperature. We were about to wash a guillemot which I had caught and brought in from another room.

As I firmly held the bird on either side of its body, Paul caught its head in such a way that the beak could not do any damage and deftly placed the rubber tube over its beak so that it could not peck. Jane Lacey entered the room suitably dressed in suit and high heels with her radio pack in a large case slung from her shoulder. With microphone in hand, she saw what we were doing.

'Oh, wonderful, just what I wanted', she said as she made her way over to us. 'Can I just interview you as you wash him? Isn't he sweet?' she cooed at the bird, glancing at Paul.

Now if she had been one of the blonde attractive interviewers that had been with the many television crews following the disaster, she may have had a better response, but pushing his glasses back up his nose, Paul explained to her that hopefully there would not be much noise to this process to assist the atmosphere of a radio interview.

'Don't worry about that,' she said, waving her hand (which was not exactly helping the bird), 'I can explain everything as you do it.'

'Fine', said Paul. 'But I really want to get on with this bird, so you carry on.'

'It's going out live', she explained – a look of horror washed over Paul's face. 'I'll just take your voice level. Now,' she said, pushing the microphone under Paul's nose, 'what did you have for breakfast?'

Paul stopped soaping the guillemot's head. 'I'm sorry, but what has that got to do . . . ?'

Looking slightly fractious as time was running out, 'I know, I know, I just want you to say something so that I can get your voice level', she answered.

'But I didn't have any breakfast', quipped Paul.

'Just give me your name and address', she sighed in exasperation. Paul conceded.

Quickly adjusting her dial for volume, she smiled sweetly and listened intently on her earphones, waiting for her cue from the radio station.

By now Paul was washing the back of the bird and all you could see was a sink full of foam and the head complete with orange rubber tube on its beak rising above it.

'I'm here at the West Hatch RSPCA Wildlife Unit, where staff are busy washing the hundreds of oiled birds that have been brought to this Centre. This is Paul Kennedy of the RSPCA who is washing a bird at this moment with his colleague – Hello, Paul', ran the interview.

'Hello', said Paul to the black instrument shoved in his face, trying to see the bird underneath it.

'Now this is really exciting,' enthused Jane to the audience listening, 'the bird is completely immersed under the water to give it a good wash . . .'

Horrified, both Paul and I stared down at the bird, making sure the bird's head was well above the water.

' . . . scrubbing hard to remove all the oil . . .' she continued.

Leaning forward I whispered into Paul's ear – 'So that's why we put the tube on the beak – so that they can breathe under the water, like a scuba tube!'

. . . so that they can breathe under the water, like a scuba tube!

I only hope that the giggling sounded more like gurgling, for her sake, as for the rest of the interview neither of us was able to speak, through laughing.

What use is that kind of information that she was giving? She had taken neither the time nor the interest to find out what was really happening. First you are shown the disaster on screen and then the nice bits of how we are all working hard getting them all better. Why don't they show the pile of dead ones that didn't make it, or the fact that three months later the staff were still dealing with the problem – but by then, nobody wants to know – that's old news. Forty per cent of all the oiled birds admitted to West Hatch were ringed and released.

Still they are happy to revive the story when experts say that it is all a waste of time, that the percentage of birds that survive when put back is so low that all the effort is useless. This despite dead birds being found four years later whose rings prove they have survived that long.

Even if the percentage is low – what shall we do at the next disaster? Collect them all up in black bags and say – what a shame, but it's not worth the bother? If people are prepared to put the effort in, and there's plenty of them, societies such as the RSPCA have the cash to fund the work – that's what they are there for, it's why we donate to them, and anyway, expenses will be billed against the insurers of the ship. Maybe, if the bills are big enough, ships may install more protective measures for cargoes of oil, and just maybe, stringent rules of dispensing commodities would be enforced more diligently.

For the very few that we are told eventually survive and live another day, we have a duty to do what we can for them. I applaud everyone who worked so hard during that difficult time. As far as I'm concerned, they did a damn good job.

3

Milking a Badger

My own personal involvement with the oiled birds finished fairly soon after the first two weeks, as I was needed elsewhere. A small badger cub was found by a sett that had been dug by baiters. The straight sides of the holes leading to the chambers of the once secure home were scored with spade marks. With the adult animals taken away, a small three-week-old cub had been left behind and was found crying through hunger, unable to understand why his mother had not returned to protect and feed him.

The badger cub season had started. We expect to get orphan badger cubs any time from February onwards, as badgers have delayed implantation and it is usually February or March that they are born – but here we were still just in January with the first cub on its way. It had been reported to the RSPCA in Bristol, and it would not be long before the Inspector would arrive with the cub, so I fetched the incubator and put it in the kitchen ready to start warming.

The fact that this cub was coming from Bristol reminded me of a school party that came to our Centre. Badger baiting is a 'sport' that is usually associated with Wales and Yorkshire, although it does occur in other towns, but I was horrified when a teacher brought a class out to us from Bristol in 1993 wanting them to see a live badger. He confided in me that he knew that two of the children's parents were involved with badger baiting in the city and he wanted to educate the children as to the cruelty of this sport and to teach them respect for animals. They were able to meet my Bluebell and were thrilled at getting so close. I sincerely hope that none of those children were involved in this incident.

The white van turned into the yard. Hushing the dogs to stop barking, I met the Inspector who carried the cardboard box into the kitchen. Opening the lid, I peered inside to see a small black and white body wrapped in a soft towel. He whickered at the disturbance, turning his head which was muddy from where he had scrabbled along the ground.

His eyes were tightly shut, and would be for another two weeks, for badger cubs mature very slowly and their eyes and ears remain closed for the first five weeks of life. But his sense of smell was telling him of his strange surroundings and he cried in distress. Why do I never tire of baby badgers? They are just so enchanting – forget the night-time feeds, the heartache when things go wrong, it is so easy to understand why individuals want to keep a badger cub if they rear one. The fact that this black and white mammal, looking more like a teddy bear, is going to grow into a very strong badger is the furthermost thought from your mind. Wrapping him in the towel that he was used to, I cradled him in my arms oblivious of the shiny fleas running through the short silvery fur.

'What I'd give to catch those bastards . . .' said the Inspector angrily. 'Still, at least that little cub is in the best place.' He smiled; like him, I failed to understand how people can be so cruel. 'I must be off – see you again soon, no doubt!' he said, and waving goodbye, he was gone.

Sitting with the cub on my lap, I carefully examined him. Condition-wise he was very healthy. The mud would soon dry and clean away from his fur. There seemed to be no injuries, so hopefully the cub was further down in a deeper chamber and had escaped the attack. I could not bear to think of where the rest of his family were now – whatever their fate, I prayed their end would be quick. At least the Inspector would go back regularly to make sure no more cubs were left behind, but he was fairly sure that this was a single.

Squirming in the warmth of my body, the cub twisted on to his back, his soft paws twitching as he slept. Even now the shiny claws showed although they were pale and fine, belying the strong, long powerful claws that they would become ready for a lifestyle of digging.

I am painfully reminded of Bluebell, how she came to me with Primrose and Willow at the age of only five weeks, and the many cubs that had followed.

'You', I said to the little cub, 'will have a special name. You're the first cub since my Bluebell died. I'm going to call you Glade, like a clearing in a forest after an old tree dies and new growth starts. You are my new beginning.'

I held him up, his small body filling my cupped hands. 'Hmm, must do something about the fleas!' I murmured. 'But at the moment, you get some sleep.'

Placing him on to the fleece in the incubator with his old towel, I checked the temperature and curved the towel around him. With a slight whimper at being moved, Glade soon settled and continued to sleep.

'Where is he?!', said Debbie, bursting in.

Debbie is our manageress and is in her twenties, having come to us originally as a volunteer. She has been with us for several years now, having herself spent a year in Australia and she was green with envy at Simon being out there. 'I'd heard the cub had arrived – let me have a look', she pleaded.

We try to restrict contact with the cubs as much as possible, and Debbie will usually be the only one other than me who will do feeds with the orphans. That's why we usually rear them in my kitchen, and even the staff very rarely get to see them. Our visitors, as you can imagine, are always very interested in the badger cubs which is why we have closed circuit television and cameras, so that these can capture the cubs for people to see without disturbing them in any way. The more close contact with humans, the more difficult it is for badgers to revert to being wild – even with limited contact, some cubs will occasionally remain too tame. Debbie, like me, is fond of badgers but is also very good with bats and does most of our baby bat rearing.

Looking through the perspex lid of the incubator, she could just see his head and front paws poking out from the towel.

'Ohhh! Isn't he lovely', she purred (not in the least a professional attitude!). 'Have you thought of a name for him yet?'

'Yes,' I said definitely, 'I'm calling him Glade.'

Laughing, she remarked, 'That sounds like an air freshener!'

'Glade it is', I replied smiling, and explained my reason. Little did I know just how special he was to become.

It was to be a year of early cubs. A local farmer, Jeff Newton, called into the office while I was doing some paperwork. His farm is only down in the village of East Huntspill, which is about a mile from our home. Jeff had noticed a badger lying on her side near his tractor and, at first, thought she was dead, but on his taking a closer look, she roused herself and ran behind some pallets leaning against the side of an old wooden shed.

He went on to feed some calves that he was keeping in a nearby barn, and whilst in there heard some whimpering coming from the hay feeder.

'I don't know what badger cubs sound like, but it's definitely something quite young that is crying and I think you'd better come and have a look', said Jeff.

All our local farmers know my interest in badgers and most of them, given healthy badgers in not too great a number, are quite happy to have them on their land. Jeff was no exception and was concerned that there was obviously something wrong with the badger that he had seen.

Calling Debbie to help me, we arranged to get the equipment together and meet Jeff down at his farm. It is always best to go equipped for any event (without going overboard) and we eventually arrived with badger cage, grasper, net and blankets.

Driving past the farmhouse, round to the cows, I was reminded of how different our farm now looks. Not that Jeff's farm is untidy, but the very fact of being a farm means that there is machinery parked in various places, brambles covering broken articles long ago discarded and forgotten, tyres banked against a wall until needed, and stacked wood that always 'comes in handy' at odd times. Our visitors expect the farm to be scrupulously clean and the presence of too much mud (let alone that awful stuff called dung) would soon have the high-heeled country lover complaining of the conditions.

Parking near the shed, Jeff indicated where the badger was hiding behind the pallets. She was still there and very frightened. Pulling back from where she was, we assessed the situation. If you stay looking at a wild animal it will panic and often run away, which we definitely did not want to happen. So leaving her quietly where she was, Jeff took us round to the hay feeder and, yes, it was the sound of small badger cubs. I was loath, at this time, to part the hay and see where they were.

The first priority was to catch the badger. If it was a sow, and these cubs belonged to her, there must be a reason why she was not lying up with them. Placing the cage open-ended, blocking one end of the pallets, I left Debbie to slide the door down if the badger ran in. We had covered it with a blanket, to encourage her to run into what appeared to be a sheltered hole.

Climbing over a wooden gate and struggling past old pieces of machinery, I made my way to the other side of the pallets. I had a grasper in my hand, a long pole with a loop at the end which can be useful in certain situations. I must admit, I am loath to use them as restricting a badger in a tightened noose can cause severe stress, but if the alternative is not to catch the badger, then I would use it. I also had a blanket to put in front of me, in case, with bravado, she opted to run towards me instead of the cage.

It is very difficult in these situations to move in and block all other forms of exit, but the pallets were closely stacked and it was impossible for her to work her way through the sides, so she only had two options. She chose the cage. Hesitating just in front of the cage door, the badger looked back, but the sight of me moving nearer to her was enough to motivate her to try and hide in the cage. Quickly sliding the door, as soon as the badger entered the cage, Debbie had her confined. The most difficult part was over. Leaving the blanket over the cage to minimalise any stress the badger may have been feeling, we lifted the cage into the back of the car. I was pretty sure it was a sow from the shape of her head (a boar's head is much broader). She was now just lying in the cage, unconcerned by her new surroundings, which I thought was a certain indicator that she was not feeling at all well.

Jeff, Debbie and I made our way to the hay to look at what was making the noise. Parting the hay, we saw three incredibly small pink forms emitting calls that one would have thought were impossible from such tiny animals. These little badger cubs could only be about 24 hours old.

Our immediate thought was that perhaps the sow was having difficulty giving birth to another cub so we decided to take her straight to the vet. Carefully picking the cubs up in the hay that they lay in, we tried not to touch them with our hands. If possible, the best chance these cubs had was to be put back with the mother.

With Debbie cradling her precious cargo in a blanket on her lap, I quickly rang through to Liz, our vet, on the mobile. Luck was with us, as she was at the surgery. Jeff wished us luck and we thanked him for getting in touch with us. We were soon on our way to the vets' surgery which was only 15 minutes away in Bridgwater.

Lifting the cage onto the examination table, Liz looked at the badger.

'You've been in the wars, old girl', she commented, seeing that from past fights both her ears were missing and her nose had a scar from a deep wound. This was probably why the sow had chosen to have her cubs in the hay feeder. Usually only the dominant female will have cubs in a sett, and should another sow become pregnant, she will often choose to have her cubs away from the sett as the dominant sow would sometimes kill them.

'Let's have a look at her then', said Liz, sliding out the rod that secured the top lid to the cage. As I was covering the sow's head with my leather gauntlets, Liz was confident enough to feel down the badger's body and move her limbs. The badger offered no resistance. 'I think you're right, Pauline, I think we need to x-ray and find out what's going on inside – and the quicker we can move the better.' Calling to the nurse to prepare the x-ray machine, Liz opened the drawer of a cabinet to find some anaesthetic to make the sow sleepy and allow us to handle her better.

Care has to be taken with anaesthetic as it is not only the weight of the animal but also its condition that has to be taken into account in the calculation of the dosage. With all Liz's experience with our badgers, I was confident of her actions. It was not long before the sow was breathing deeply and not responding to touch.

Sliding a muzzle over the badger's face, Liz secured the catch at the side of the head. She had already learnt her lesson as to the quick reactions of a semi-conscious badger and was not going to tempt fate again. To be fair, I have never known a badger attempt to bite unless in a restrained situation, and the only vets that I know of that have been bitten, have experienced this whilst the animal has been in a confused state of anaesthetic.

Moving her on to the x-ray table, Liz quickly positioned the sow using small weighted bags of sand which hold the body as required whilst the x-ray is being taken. She went out of the room while the picture was being taken and then the nurse put it into the machine to develop. Liz moved the badger into another position for a further x-ray. At the same time she examined the condition of the badger, looking at her gums and checking her hydration, judging her age by her teeth and looking at their wear and tear, and finally checking under her tail for birth fluids and signs of infection.

Another click as the second x-ray is taken, and the machine drones as it whirrs into action. Moving the sow to recovery position, Liz played with the badger's feet. 'I love their feet, their pads are so soft', she said, screwing up her nose in delight. So nice to have such a caring vet as far as badgers are concerned.

Speed is of the essence, and soon the film is clipped to the lighted box for Liz to find out exactly what is wrong with our casualty. Changing to the next picture, Liz mused: 'Right, I don't think we are looking at anything too serious here, the womb is empty. She's suffering with a womb infection – there's some nasty smelling fluids under her tail and she has some territorial bite wounds. I'd have to say that she is quite an old badger so probably the infection has just taken her over, giving her a high temperature, and leaving her feeling very ill and weak. I think with antibiotics, and T.L.C., she should make it.'

Everyone was pleased – by now we had other vets in the room being nosey, most of the nurses and Debbie and I – and we all breathed a sigh of relief.

'What about the cubs?' said Debbie, still holding them to keep them warm.

'Well, let's give them a feed while the sow's asleep – the anaesthetic will not have affected the milk yet and anyway, it's the only chance we'll get', said Liz. So the cubs, still wrapped in hay, were latched to the nipples of the sow and allowed to feed.

The nurses were amazed at how small the cubs were. A mere 4 or 5 inches long, they only weighed just under 200 grammes. Their pink bodies shimmered with grey fur that was starting to come through. Only faintly could you see the dark stripes on their heads that were to become the distinctive black and white face that everyone knows.

'There's still a long way to go', remarked Liz. 'Due to her age, she may not produce enough milk.'

'She may not accept the cubs either', I replied. 'Perhaps if you leave the muzzle on and don't reverse the anaesthetic, as we usually do, she'll stay sleepy and come round slowly in the casualty pen with the cubs, which might help.'

'Yes,' said Liz, 'that should work. I'll just take a blood sample and give her the antibiotic and you can get going with her before she comes round.'

'You ought to try and get a sample of her milk', I reminded Liz. We had been trying for some time to get badger milk analysed to find out its true composition and therefore ensure that the milk substitute that we use is the correct balance for them.

Knowing I was right, she scolded me, 'The things I do for you, Pauline Kidner! If ever this gets out that I have been milking a badger, I'll never live it down.'

However, the sow had very little milk and Liz was only able to get a very small sample. We just hoped it was enough.

'If ever this gets out that I have been milking a badger . . .'

Placing her back in the cage, we were keen to get going. This was a new situation for us and we were unsure as to what was going to happen. I think badgers are more amenable to disturbance, in that I doubt that they would normally eat their young as would happen particularly with rabbits. However, I was not at all sure of what this sow would think of waking up in a casualty pen, which is a far cry from the old shed where she gave birth.

We collected some more of the hay from the shed where the cubs had been born and made a bed in the corner of the pen. Quietly lying her on the hay, she continued to sleep. We placed the three small cubs by her, and naturally they wriggled against her stomach, safe in the protection of the curve of her body. They disappeared from view and, apart from a few whimpers and squeaks, all fell silent. Now, there was nothing more that we could do, but watch. Luckily Alan Gory, a volunteer who has proved helpful with setting up alarms and surveillance equipment, was on hand and he rigged up a camera so that we did not even have to go into the casualty pen area, opening doors and possibly disturbing her through noise: we could watch from a monitor outside.

We watched her intently, wondering if we were doing the right thing. Would it have been better to have just given her one cub and see if she took to that first? How bad were we going to feel if she turned round and killed them all? It was a question of wait and see. At least by leaving the muzzle on, we had avoided the immediate danger of her killing the cubs when she came round, but I wasn't looking forward to taking the muzzle off, nor to giving her the daily injections that Liz had given me to administer to her. Still, let's take one thing at a time.

A ripple of a shiver ran down the sow's body, and slowly she lifted her head. She listened. The movement caused the cubs to start to whimper and immediately she was distracted from her surroundings to check if her cubs were there. As she was still sleepy the muzzle caused no discomfort, and with one more look around her pen, she drifted back to sleep.

Another half an hour and I felt the time had come to take the muzzle off. Climbing slowly into the pen, I shielded myself with a folded blanket with which I deftly covered the sow and cubs completely. Feeling through the blanket, I found her head and keeping my hand there to sense any movement, I turned back the blanket until I found the muzzle clasp. As I undid the muzzle and slid it away, the sow remained still. Slowly lifting the blanket, talking to her as I did it, I moved back to the door. Her eyes followed me but she made no attempt to move. Jumping slightly at the noise of the bolt going across the door as I shut it, she nuzzled between her paws at the cubs. The interaction caused an outburst of whickering and a tiny tail and back legs came into view as the responding cub lifted the lower part of its body to scent its mother by emitting musk from its anal gland. A more natural sight would be hard to find. Mum and babies looked to be doing well!

Mandy Phillips, who was then our Animal Supervisor, was living with us at the time and we agreed to take it in turns to check up on the sow and cubs every hour. It was after Mandy's turn that she came running up. 'It's no good, she's tossing the cubs around in the straw', she called out, running up the stairs.

'Wait a minute,' I said, calming her down, 'what happened?'

She explained that while she was watching, the sow moved away from the cubs to shake and stretch and then went to return to the bed. The sow had tossed the straw and the cubs up in the air and Mandy was sure that she was going to hurt them.

'I'm sure', I confided in her, 'that when we go down, she will be curled up with them safe and sound.' And we both quickly made our way down to the pens. I had seen Bluebell with her cubs that were born in the observation sett, and another sow called Snowdrop who had produced cubs, acting in this way before. Just like pigs, they root the bedding and it all goes in the air – straw, cubs, everything! Then very slowly, going down on their front shoulder first, they lie down, taking great care that they do not lie on top of piglet or cub. Once the mother is on her side, the babes will make their way to the stomach of the animal, and usually, given the chance, will start to feed. Just as I thought, the sounds of contentment told the story of the whole situation. The sow was lying quietly on her side and the small baby sounds of squeaking coming from the straw made me think that there were some full tummies.

Having seen the small cubs, when I went back to feeding Glade, he seemed enormous. Being that much older than the three and probably a single cub at that, he was enjoying his bottles and had become quite a chunky little fellow. Glade being the first cub that we had knowingly had from a digging incident, it was surprising that we were about to get another. Just like buses, they all come together . . .

Taffy

Badger group members from Glamorgan rang late on a Sunday evening to ask if I could take a very small cub found near a sett that had been dug. Far too small to be of any use to the digger, the cub had been discarded on top of the spoil by the sett entrance. Although it would be well into the night by the time they reached me, they arranged to drive straight over with it.

'Who was that ringing on a Sunday night?' asked Derek, wandering into the kitchen from the lounge where he had been reading the newspaper.

I explained what had happened as Derek switched on the kettle to make a cup of coffee. 'Here we go again,' he complained, 'badgers all over the house – you don't realise how lucky you are having me put up with all this every year.'

Derek does not like to get involved with the cubs at all, but I suppose he does have a point. I graciously smiled. 'So lucky!' I reiterated.

Sunday is the one day that Derek does not like to have his meal and evening interrupted. By no means does this have a religious connotation on his part, he just likes it to be as quiet as possible. He is therefore somewhat curt if people ring up for what he considers to be 'unnecessary calls' on a Sunday.

This did catch him out one day, as last year he was called out to an injured badger in a lady's garden. It was fairly late, and once he had captured the badger, the lady said how grateful she was. She explained that she could not afford to give him a donation but mentioned that she knew Valerie Singleton (of 'Blue Peter' fame) and when she saw her next, she would ask her if she would help us. Derek said that it was very kind of her and not to worry about the donation, and went on his way.

The badger was duly installed and was undergoing treatment. At quarter to ten the next Sunday night, the telephone rang and Derek was the one to answer. I could tell from the expression of eyes rolling to the ceiling that this was 'an unnecessary Sunday telephone call', and to start with Derek's comments were very short. But suddenly he was enthusing over our work and going into great detail as to the progress of the badger that he had rescued. Great descriptions of our charity and worthwhile work were tripping off his tongue.

Bemused, I just had to stay to find out *who* he was talking to.

'Thank you very much for calling', he was finishing; 'no, you can call any time you like' he said, smiling down the phone.

'Well!', I exclaimed, 'Who on earth was that to be spoken to so nicely on a Sunday evening?'

It was Valerie Singleton! She has since become one of our patrons and supports us in many ways, for which we are very grateful. So you now know – don't ring on Sunday unless you're famous!

Glamorgan badger group obviously weren't famous, because by the time they got to us Derek had gone to bed! And what a sad sight the small cub made. Under a week old, with dog bite wounds to his side where he had been tossed about, the tiny cub still quivered despite being nursed so caringly by Helen in the car. Pathetically thin, he had been without food for some time, so using a small syringe with a teat on the end, I offered him some lectade water. If an orphan has been without food for some time, it is not always a good thing to offer them milk straightaway as they will be very thirsty, and often too much rich food at once will give them a tummy upset and you can end up with a severely dehydrated animal. Lectades are a combination of water and minerals that will replace desperately needed fluids without upsetting the gut, which can often lead to diarrhoea and therefore more fluid loss.

There are also many types of milk that you can use for wildlife – definitely not cow's milk – and if you haven't got the right milk, you are often better to give water with just a pinch of salt and sugar until you can get the right fluids.

I gently pushed the plunger on the syringe, and the warm liquid trickled into the small cub's mouth. He swallowed. Sensing that more fluid was to follow, he curled his tongue around the teat and latched on. Eager for more, he started to suck and he complained each time I removed the syringe to refill. At this stage, he was still too small to drink from a bottle. Gradually his sucking slowed, and he fell asleep with just the tip of his pink tongue sticking out from his mouth.

Giving him back to Helen to hold now that he was more content, while I made coffee, they told me the background to him being found. I was ashamed to hear that in Glamorgan, on average, they will lose two or three setts every weekend to diggers. So many of the general public think that digging is an archaic tradition that no longer takes place – how little they know! The police do all they can to help the badger groups but, with limited funding, wildlife persecution tends to be quite low in the order of priorities.

My new cub already has a name: Taffy – what else for a Welsh badger? Placed in his warm bed, separate from Glade, Taffy was left to sleep. Wishing the Glamorgan badger group members a safe journey home, I switched off the outside lights. Time to crawl into bed for a few hours before the next feed is due.

The following morning, we were to get a call from a local car auction near the Dunball roundabout, just outside Bridgwater. It is a huge auction hall where company cars, lorries and bankrupt stock are sold. The vehicles are all in lines at the back of the auction ring, where you can start the engines and view them. As the place is so large it has restaurant and seating facilities where you can await the sale of a vehicle that you may be interested in. All around the perimeter of this huge compound, as you can imagine, are tall security fences all monitored by security men with the aid of closed circuit cameras. Halfway through the night, a badger had been seen excavating his way into the compound and was now known to be curled up asleep under one of the hundreds of cars queued up to go in the auction ring.

They wanted us to remove the badger, and to be as quick as possible as they had already started to sell and lines of cars were already on the move. This time Derek was to come with me; again badger cage, grasper, leather gauntlets and net were taken. The net, in fact, is a large landing net meant for fishing, which we have used very successfully on many occasions particularly if the badger is 'on the run'.

Discussing the situation as we drove there, Derek and I thought that it would probably be a male badger. At this time of year we often get called out to males that have been beaten up, as while the sows have their cubs, the males are evicted from the setts and spend their time defending their territory. Sometimes, when we catch them, if the male is very old with large wounds, we would consider putting them down. This usually happens because a younger male is fighting for the territory, and in nature these old males, once badly injured, go away to die. If treated and returned to their homes it is possible they will be beaten up all over again, and sadly we have proved this to happen in the past.

At other times it can be a young boar badger, probably a yearling, that has been frightened off by a belligerent male, and if left alone, they will wander back when the coast is clear.

On arrival at the entrance gates, our van with the 'badger logo' on the side was immediately recognised, and we were waved in. The security man walked over and explained that he had watched the badger dig his way in and make his way to the west end of the car park – he would show us where. Directing us to follow his car, he took us to the back of the auction where we faced a complete sea of lines and lines of cars waiting to go through the auction.

'He's somewhere in there', he waved helpfully, his arm sweeping the total expanse of the car park.

'You are sure he's still in there, aren't you?' asked Derek – not given to wasting time on fool's errands.

'Oh, yes,' the security man nodded, 'he was seen just now running from one line of cars to another – he's definitely there.'

Leaving us, as people do, with complete faith that you can handle the situation, he drove back to his nice warm office. It was cold, it was wet and there were a lot of people just milling around. The only thing we could do was to get down on our hands and knees at the end of every row of cars and see if we could find a badger.

Derek had the grasper and I had the net. At the first row of cars that I came to, mystified prospective buyers watched as I knelt looking under the line of cars.

'You won't catch any fish under there' was the droll remark from an inquisitive man.

I smiled and got up. 'No, I don't suppose I will', I replied.

'What are you looking for?' another man asked.

'A badger', I answered, moving away quickly before I had to explain any more.

By the time I had been told that 'I wouldn't find any fish under there' for the fifth time, the joke was wearing thin. My trousers were getting wetter and wetter and not a black and white face in sight.

'There he is', Derek hollered as the badger, suddenly surprised by Derek squatting by the car, had made a break for it and run between the cars. A crowd of people that had gathered together, intrigued at what was going on, parted with screams as the poor terrified badger ran through them and then apparently disappeared into thin air. No one saw where he went in all the excitement.

. . . the badger made a break for it . . .

Even with Derek and I running at full pace to get to the row of
cars nearest the commotion, we were still no further forward in
the capture of the badger – although we were now pretty sure that
he was a completely healthy young male that had dug his way in
for a peaceful night away from all the family arguments!

Time was running out as more and more cars had moved to
the auction ring, but at least there was now less cover in the way
of parked vehicles for the badger to hide under. By now we had
plenty of helpers, but it was obvious that when the time came to
try to catch the poor animal, it was going to be practically
impossible in such an open situation. When at last the badger
was located, he immediately took his chance and headed unfortunately for the auction ring, where he did two laps of honour
before shooting off in the opposite direction.

It was a long time since I had run so fast and my age was
beginning to tell! Behind me, Derek was gasping too. The 'lost
brock' suddenly found his bearings and made for his hole under
the fence where he had entered the night before. Wriggling under
as fast as he could, he disappeared back home for a sleep after his
adventurous night, to the sound of applause from the ever-larger
watching crowd that had gathered to see what all the excitement
was about.

Two very pink-faced, tired people, filthy from crawling under cars, made their way back to the van. When people ask me why I love badgers, there are times that I have to admit that I'm not really sure, and Derek would probably clarify his feelings quite eloquently!

Glade seemed to be the only one who was not giving me any worries. Whilst the sow with the cubs was being very good about being injected, she was not drinking or eating. She looked well and the cubs seemed to be feeding and appeared contented, but I was concerned that if she did not start to eat soon, her milk would fail and we would have all sorts of problems. However, badgers can go a very long period of time without feeding, so I decided to leave the sow at least for a week. She had been named Carey after Care For The Wild International, a national charity that works very hard for wildlife across the world. Their charity had given us money towards our new casualty pens and are always very supportive of our work.

I was in a dilemma over Taffy, as since putting him on to Complan, which we have always used to rear badger cubs in the past, he had come out with a severe allergy and was becoming very weak. It is always an added responsibility when you know that the individuals who brought the cub in to you will want to know how it is progressing, and it always seems to be these that you have problems with – never the cub that has been brought in at death's door by someone who was out walking and who, although they take the care to bring them in, never bother to ring and see if they survive. They're the ones that usually make it!

Putting him yet again on to lectades, Liz suggested an American milk powder available for puppies, called Esbilac. It is quite expensive but appeared to have good results with wildlife orphans, so we ordered some. Sadly, the milk that Liz had tried to express out of Carey had not been enough to analyse so we still do not know the compound of badger milk. Until the milk powder arrived, little and often of the lectade was the best I could do for Taffy, but I had real worries that I might be losing him.

Not so the hunk! Glade, now with eyes open, was beginning to play and it would soon be very important that he was put with a similar cub for company. Meanwhile he was allowed to play with Murray, our dog. Murray is a cross between an Alsatian and a Doberman, and being male, it is surprising that his temperament is so maternal. He is absolutely brilliant with very small animals, even getting down on the floor to be able to mother baby rabbits.

Murray played very gently with Glade, despite appearing enormous to him. This gutsy little badger cub soon learnt that he could bite Murray's jowls and paws if the play got a bit rough and he could get his own back. Some think it is wrong to get badgers used to playing with dogs, but our other dog, Barney, dislikes badger cubs intensely and the cubs soon learn which dog is a friend and which is an enemy.

Now too big for the incubator, Glade had moved into the kitchen cubby-hole, which is an area in the kitchen that has a board in front to contain any cubs inside. A heat lamp kept him warm, and when it was playtime he was allowed out into the rest of the kitchen. Now quarry tiled, my kitchen is badger cub proof, which makes life a lot easier than in the days when stone animals had to placed strategically around the lino floor to stop the cubs from digging it up!

Glade did not have too long to wait before he was joined by other cubs. Poppy and Flora were to arrive within two days of each other. Poppy had been found wandering above ground. Although six or seven weeks old, she was still too young to be out on her own and certainly was not weaned. Often the mother is killed on the road, and when she fails to return, cubs will come up above ground looking for their mother and a source of food. Poppy had been discovered by a walker who had contacted a badger group member, who in turn brought her to us.

We do most of the cub rearing for the West Hatch RSPCA wildlife centre, so when cubs are taken in by the Inspectors, they usually come through to us. Flora came from a report of cubs being snared, but when the Inspector arrived on the scene, it was clear what had really happened. Sadly, a pregnant sow had taken a bundle of nylon string down into the sett as bedding for her birth chamber. She had given birth, but as her two cubs had grown they had slowly become tangled in the string; being nylon, and therefore unbreakable, it had gradually strangled one cub and eventually killed it. As the body decomposed, the sow dragged the bedding out of the sett with the dead cub caught up inside it – but the other cub, also tangled in the string, was still alive. The string had caused huge circular injuries across the small female cub's body as it had burnt the skin with friction and then caused deep cuts to her body and to the side of her head.

Freeing her from the string, the Inspector placed her in a carrier and disposed of the dead cub and the string so that it would cause no further injuries. Baling twine used for hay and straw is specially designed not to rot, but when frayed, the fine strands can often catch around the limbs of mammals and even small birds' feet, eventually cutting into them so deeply that the limb dies from oxygen starvation and will rot off. If ever there was a good example to our staff, whom we constantly reprimand for leaving string lying around, this was surely it.

Amazingly, apart from bathing the little cub's wounds and giving her antibiotic, there was little that needed to be done for Flora and she was soon a bouncing healthy cub as her wounds healed, and she became as keen to play as Poppy and Glade.

Taffy was also by this time beginning to get over his very traumatic start to life. The Esbilac milk was being used for all the cubs and they were thriving on it. Where all his skin had flaked away, the new fur was coming through and even where the dog bite wounds had been, the scars could hardly be seen on Taffy's body now. At five weeks old, his eyes were just starting to open and the bright black pupils glinted in the corners of his eyes as the skin started to pull apart.

I was still very concerned for Carey. She had failed to eat and drink for two weeks, but then at last she started to drink. However, she still refused to feed. I did try to syringe feed her a couple of times with some Complan, honey and egg, which is usually taken quite readily by badgers, but she really wasn't that bothered. She continued to look well and the cubs were growing, although nothing like the orphan cubs in the kitchen who were demonstrating how cubs can pile on the weight when food is readily available! But Carey's cubs still looked healthy so we left her alone.

I suppose when you think about it, in the first two weeks, the sow is cleaning up after the cubs while she feeds them so a certain amount of protein must be re-ingested. And to leave very small cubs in a sett unprotected while the mother looks for food would leave them very much at risk, and anyway I doubt that the sow would be able to find enough food in a short time to replace the energy required in moving – so doubtless there is little movement or feeding in the early days after giving birth in the natural environment.

We were putting lectade in Carey's water, so this would have been replacing natural minerals, and energy of course. She was also under a heat lamp, so was using up little personal energy to keep herself warm. However, I was greatly relieved when, after four weeks of fresh food being put in every day, I found that the peanuts had disappeared from the top of the food. The next night all the food disappeared and from then on she fed regularly.

It is a fine balance to try and get things right, to know when to leave things alone and, on other occasions, when not to allow certain situations to go on. If you get it wrong, you feel awful. If it turns out right, you feel great. It all seemed to be going well – yes, it was going to be a good year!

4

Prison Talk

It is very rare that a person can tell you exactly when a badger cub was born, but later that spring that's just what happened. At the beginning of April, we had a telephone call from a riding stable in Wiltshire. They had an indoor arena for riding lessons and all around the perimeter of the arena were wooden boards behind which hay was stored, between the boards and the walls.

Mrs Christian, the owner, told me that on several occasions they would see badgers lying up in the hay, and at the beginning of the previous week she had heard some squeaking.

Peering over the sides of the board, she noticed a badger with four newly born cubs. Whilst fairly indifferent to wildlife, she had no problems with them being there and left them alone.

A few days later, however, she noticed that the sow had moved further along the wall and had only taken three of the four cubs with her. The remaining cub was crying at being deserted. Loath to interfere, Mrs Christian had left it alone, thinking that in time the sow would return for it. However, by the third day, the cub was still neglected and the crying was very much weaker, so she took the cub indoors and telephoned for help.

She had no desire to look after the cub, but neither did she want to see it suffer so she asked if we would take it. Driving straight down there, as we were concerned at the period of time that the cub had been without food, Derek and I arrived in early evening, having been given very good instructions as to how to get there. Taking us into their house, it was obvious to see their interest in horses. Rosettes of all colours and sizes adorned the mantelpiece, together with many cups and trophies that had been won over the years.

It was a lovely welcoming cottage, decorated very tastefully, and yet giving an element of relaxation and comfort. Mrs Christian had wrapped the cub up in an old towel with a hot water bottle, and despite his unhappy start to life he looked very well. Mrs Christian and her family could not understand why the cub had been deserted.

Orphans are very difficult to analyse straight away. Very often the mother is aware of a genetic defect and will abandon a baby rather than waste energy on rearing a non-viable animal. In this case the cub went on to grow into a healthy animal, so I think the explanation was probably that the sow realised that she only had enough milk for three cubs, and in nature, it is better to rear three healthy cubs than to rear four sickly, weak ones that would be unlikely to survive for very long.

The family were grateful that we were going to look after this very small badger cub, which was only just a week old, but they never contacted us again to see if he survived. Still, at least they bothered to do something about the little cub. Only last year an adult badger was seen in a farmyard lying on its side, obviously ill. It was nearly a week before anyone thought to let a vet know, by which time it was too late and the badger died soon after. I know people will have different interests and I am sure that many do not share my love of animals. But for some odd reason, wildlife is perceived not to require, or even be valued enough to be given, veterinary treatment – do people really think that they don't feel pain?

The incubator was brought out again for this tiny cub's arrival back at the farm. Taffy, now a bouncing six-week-old cub, had joined the big guys in the cubby-hole and the freedom of the kitchen floor. Three-hourly feeds were to start again, just as the older cubs were reducing in feeds and life was getting easier! With such a tiny cub, it was unlikely, I thought, that we would get another so young and it would be a long time before he would have a friend to join him.

As you can imagine, the cub was very pleased to get a feed of lectade, and I was happy with the thoughts of his progress now that we were using the new milk that seemed to suit the small cubs so well. Named Barley, the small cub fed well and fell asleep, but his tiny whimpers continued, almost as natural as breathing – he was obviously still distressed at the thought of being left alone again. I gave him a tiny teddy bear to cuddle up to, but the whimpers continued.

Glade, Flora, Poppy and Taffy were in their element with the kitchen as their play area. The smooth, quarry tiled floor meant that you could drag the rug quite easily from one side of the kitchen to the other, irrespective of whether two other cubs were fighting together on it at the same time!

Although not quite ready to wean, their interest in food was starting to show. A custard cream would be knocked round the kitchen like a puck in ice hockey, with a bevy of black and white players muscling in with their shoulders and squabbling over the biscuit. The winner would hold it in his mouth, with his head as high as possible, trying to make any attempts of snatching it away by the others impossible, only to realise that everyone else had now become interested in a roll of kitchen paper. Therefore the biscuit, by now just a bit soggy, would be dropped as the individual charged over to join the other game.

So who comes into the kitchen and treads on the soggy biscuit only to glide to the other side of the room in one easy movement – it's ice skating Derek! It's that look of split-second panic on a person's face as they lose their balance that seems so hysterically funny to the onlooker. The remark is usually, 'You have a very funny sense of humour' or 'those bleep, bleep, bleep badgers!!!!'

Barley was not to be on his own for very long after all, because a couple of nights later a very tiny cub was found on the side of the road in Dorset. Probably the mother was moving the cub to another home and, disturbed by oncoming traffic, dropped it and left the small cub behind. When discovered, the cub was cold and shivering, so it must have been on the side of the road for some time and it was unlikely that the sow was going to return.

Almost the same age as Barley, at a guess, this very small cub brought to us by the RSPCA Inspector was a little female. So once she had had all her health checks, little Ebony was able to share the incubator with Barley. He absolutely adored her, even though both still had their eyes and ears sealed; as soon as you moved Ebony out to feed, Barley would start to cry so it was easier to have them both out on my lap at the same time.

Within a week, Ebony developed a high temperature which we thought was probably from the chill of being on the road making her susceptible to an infection, and she was placed on a course of injections. It was not a good idea to keep them both together with the worry of Barley developing the same infection, but I somehow knew that if I separated them, Barley would become ill anyway – he had become so attached to this tiny female cub.

On the second day of her treatment Ebony became very lethargic, showing no interest in her feeds, and I began to think that she was close to dying. Barley was forever nuzzling her and making tiny whickering noises that were more comforting than distressing. He constantly touched her face and body with his soft padded paws and I wondered if the attention was too much for Ebony in her condition; and yet, in a way, it was almost as if he was comforting her, willing her to live. I decided to leave them together. Holding them both in my arms I trickled small feeds of lectade into Ebony's mouth, which she duly swallowed, but she made no attempt to suck for more. I just prayed that I was not risking Barley's health by leaving them together.

However, by the next morning, both cubs were as lively as each other. Just like human babies, badger cubs have this wonderful ability of being at death's door one minute and live and kicking the next. I was just so relieved that Ebony had recovered.

The 'Back to the Wild' film crew rang to ask if they could come and film the younger badger cubs for the programme. They had decided to run the story of the rearing and releasing of the badger cubs as a strand through the whole series and wanted to start with the tiny ones coming in. It always amazes me the length of time and amount of filming that has to take place in order to put together a piece that will last only a few seconds.

As we were to film the cubs indoors, lights and sound all had to be rigged up. The producer was a very nice tall man with sandy coloured hair, very easy to talk to and get on with. His name was Mike Gunton and he explained what they wanted to get from the cubs and myself, and it was just a question of talking about the cubs and their background and doing a little bit of bottle-feeding.

It all went off without too many hitches. If you can talk into a camera lens as if it is your oldest friend and can ignore the lighting man with his reflecting silver disc, also ignoring the long stick held just above your head with a microphone covered in fluffy material that looks distinctly like a dead badger, which is being controlled by the sound man frantically turning his dials to get the right volume level, not to worry about the continuity girl with her clipboard writing all sorts of notes as you speak and try to remember what the producer has just asked you to say – it's all fairly easy.

Mike and I chatted as the crew dismantled the equipment, talking about the series and finally about Mike himself. He confided that he was glad that he was working fairly close to home as his wife was due to have a baby soon.

'Not another ginger-haired sprog to be added to the world', I sarcastically remarked.

'I am not ginger-haired,' Mike stated emphatically (I'd touched a nerve!) 'I'm strawberry blond.'

I smiled but noted that he was completely serious – I changed the subject.

March and April are usually the two months in which I am not available to give talks as I know that I shall be busy with cubs. But I had promised to do two this April.

The first was a favour for a friend called Doug Woods. Doug has taught me so much over the years; he is my guru, and my only regret is that, having become so busy, I cannot share as much time with him as I would like. He has a keen interest in all kinds of wildlife throughout the world, and imparts his knowledge in such a way that it stays with you. I am sure there are many people whose lives, and even careers, have been enriched by knowing him.

Doug occasionally does talks for the men's prison at Shepton Mallet. On this occasion he realised that he was double-booked, and so was unable to attend. He asked me if I would be prepared to go and give a talk in his place. Sensing that he could well be throwing me to the lions, I agreed more from duty than keenness.

I don't think, unless you have been involved in prison life, that you are ever prepared for what a prison is like. Once I had found the place, the very fabric of the building left you in no doubt that it was secure. Going through the heavy iron gates, I reported to the reception where a security guard, complete with heavy ring of keys attached to his belt, signed me in having checked my name and reason for being there.

I was given a security pass to wear and told to wait until a Mrs Green came to collect me and take me to the wing where I would be giving the talk. Luckily the equipment was all here, I just had to bring my own slides.

Mrs Green arrived, a very pleasant, well-dressed lady, and proceeded to take me through the various corridors. She thanked me for coming to give the talk, which she was sure the prisoners would enjoy. Thinking to myself that my talk was about wildlife, I wasn't too sure as to how well this would really go.

Out from one building to another we went, each separate building requiring the opening and locking of heavy metal barred gates. Just the clunk of gate after gate being closed behind me made me realise the finality prisoners must feel when being brought to these places for a determined length of time.

We eventually reached the building we were heading for and I was shown into a room with the screen and projector already in place.

'Most of the prisoners are just finishing their lunch,' she explained, 'but they will be coming through soon – doubtless in their own time!'

She smiled and explained that these arranged talks are part of their leisure time and they usually have three options to choose from, so there may be three in the audience, there may be fifteen – it depended on how the subject suited them.

'Don't worry', she reassured me, 'if they get up and walk out. Some of them have a very limited concentration span and they do not have to remain if they become bored. But don't think that it is any reflection on you, it's just the way they are.'

My confidence was growing (!), and the palms of my hands were beginning to feel rather damp. The sound of double doors banging together announced the arrival of some of the inmates: five or six men strolled into the room. They sprawled out on the chairs, dragging vacant chairs over to put their feet up on. No one looked particularly friendly. Two more young men dashed in, having been chasing each other down the corridor, and nearly knocked the projector over.

'Come on', corrected Mrs Green. 'Let's have less noise and take your feet off those chairs, you know you're not allowed to put your feet up like that.'

Begrudgingly the feet were removed from the chairs which were kicked away.

'I'll just see if any more are coming', she said and left the room, leaving me on my own with this happy group.

The chairs were dragged back and the feet went up again on the chair seats. I had already decided that if they wanted to put their feet up – it was fine with me.

'Open the f---ing window,' growled one of the older men, 'it's bloody hot in here.'

'I don't want the f---ing window open', another commented in return.

As luck would have it, Mrs Green returned with another seven men of various ages and, ignoring all the feet up on chairs, went on to introduce me and the talk that I was about to give.

I started giving the talk, which included many slides of different species that we care for and explaining some of the injuries and difficulties that wild animals incur because of our lifestyle. My stomach stopped churning as the feeling of confrontation changed to interest, and soon there was discussion. When it came to the badgers, a couple of men had actually been involved with men who had carried out baiting but they had been disgusted at their behaviour. I can remember wondering at the reasons why so many of these men were in prison as they appeared passionately to abhor cruelty.

When we were talking about badgers I had a slide on screen that showed a territorial wound, a huge gaping wound at the rump of the animal. I explained that it was an injury caused by one badger to another. Either the badger was being fought for the territory or he had wandered on to a territory he did not belong to and was being attacked for trespassing. Questions and answers went back and forth and suddenly one of the men put up his hand. Smiling at this childlike gesture of wishing to be heard, I nodded my head at him.

'Please, Miss, can you change the slide to another one', he asked. Whoops of teasing at this request went on with plenty of laughing and barracking.

I was quite taken aback that a grown man, and especially one in prison, should ask this. The conversation may have revolved around what they would 'f---ing' like to do to people who do such things, but I never would have felt that there would be so much interest in the subject of wildlife. I did lose one person who was not taken by the subject, but otherwise it was a good hour with interested response.

All too soon a bell signalled the end of the leisure period and the men made their way out of the door, with a few stopping to thank me for coming. One even told me he was being released soon and may come to visit – mixed feelings on that one! It was certainly a talk that I shan't forget giving. I was certainly pleased when the last gate clanged behind me and I knew that at least I was back outside!

The other talk was one that I had promised to do for a ladies' group in the village of Williton, of which Auntie Gertie, Derek's mother's sister-in-law, was a member. It was an evening meeting and the weather had been dreadful all day. The weather forecast gave out warnings of storms and heavy rain for the evening and so Derek kindly offered to come with me – mainly because of the weather but also to see Auntie Gertie as well.

Having placed all the equipment in the car, early evening feeds done, we set off just as heavy rain started to fall. The wind was certainly whipping up the water that seemed to lie across most of the roads as the gutters failed to cope with the torrent of rain. Driving through Bridgwater, Derek turned the wipers to the fastest speed as the rain changed into hail.

I don't think I had ever seen rain coming down so heavy. Most of the traffic slowed as it became less and less possible to see where the road was. Crawling along slowly, cars were pulling off the road as drivers could no longer see: and other drivers were desperately trying to steer their car off the road as their engines had failed in the torrential rain. We were well out of Bridgwater by now, and with no street lights conditions were very dangerous. We discussed turning back but were aware of people who could have turned out on such an awful night and were patiently waiting for us.

Eventually the decision was made for us as we also became a casualty of the rain – our engine cut out and died. Slowly turning the car on to the verge, we finished up off the road with a car in front of us in a similar situation. Despite trying the ignition, the engine would not respond. We decided to sit and wait for a while in the hope that the warmth of the engine may dry it out and the ignition may start.

The rain didn't ease, and indeed the wind seemed to return with a vengeance with the rain striking the windscreen in gusts. After waiting a while, further tries with the ignition responded with the awful whining noise that told us that, wet or dry, the battery was now truly flat and we were not going anywhere.

'It's no good,' said Derek, after we had momentarily waited for an angel to appear – to no effect, I might add. 'I'll have to go and ring Sam.'

Sam Cook has the garage in East Huntspill and has always repaired and maintained our cars. He also has no confidence in our own vehicle maintenance track record. Good with animals, Derek has never been mechanically minded. Sam has a very dry sense of humour, with the result that he is loved by many and hated by some!

Derek had complained once to Sam that one of his engineers had told him that he had the mechanical knowledge of a slug.

'What do you think of that?' complained Derek.

'Personally,' said Sam, 'I think that comment is very unfair on a slug!'

However, Sam is very good and will respond whenever there is a problem, so it was a question of getting to a phone to call him out. The rain hit the windscreen again and Derek went on to say that there was no point in me going as I did not know the area and would not be able to find the nearest phone. Looking at the weather, I agreed that this was a very good point and thoughtfully offered to stay with the car.

Turning the collar up on his coat, Derek opened the car door which was wrenched from his hand with the force of the wind. Pulling it back, Derek eased himself out and shut the door. Trying to pull the collar of his coat further up to his ears with little success, Derek walked off in front of the car towards Cannington.

There are times when being a woman has its advantages, and I snuggled down in my seat trying to cope with the warmth in the car slowly disappearing as time went on. Derek walked on along the pavement, realising just how far it was going to be to the phone box in the next village. There was a large farm machinery place in between but that was all closed and locked up. Eventually he came to where the traffic had halted and walked alongside the line of traffic wondering what the hold-up was. He was soon to find out, as half a mile down the road, where the road dipped and then rose quite sharply, water had flooded the road to a depth of nearly two feet and cars were trying slowly to make their way through.

Already soaking, there seemed little point in worrying about the water. Derek waded through and on to the village. As he now walked past the line of traffic going the other way, people in the waiting cars kept winding their windows down to ask what the hold-up was, so it was taking a long time just to walk along the pavement as he stopped and explained to each car in turn. The whole process of walking into Cannington, reaching the telephone and returning, wading yet again through the water to the car, took just over an hour.

Meanwhile, I sat in the car watching the tail lights of the cars in the distance and wondering what the hold-up was. Eventually an RAC van pulled in front of our car and got out to assist the car in front. Typical, I thought to myself, we would be members of the AA. The man in front had had a mobile phone and had been able to obtain assistance without even getting out of the car. Lucky devil, I thought.

In what seemed to be minutes, the mechanic had opened the bonnet, wriggled a few things around, sprayed some stuff and the engine burst into life. With a wave of thanks and a glance at the line of traffic in front, the car did a U-turn and he went back the way he came – probably to his home, I moaned to myself. The mechanic then made his way over to me and I wound the window down.

'Can I help?' he asked.

'I wish', I said with a laugh; 'we belong to the AA.'

'No problem,' he said, 'woman alone, I'm not allowed to leave you without assistance. Is it the rain that stopped the car?' he questioned.

I nodded, and he asked me to pull the lever so that he could look under the bonnet. Yet again, within minutes the problem was resolved: he linked my car to his engine with jump leads and the engine was soon purring.

'Keep it running until your husband gets back, it will help dry it out', the mechanic kindly advised. 'Which way did he go?'

I explained that he knew the area better than me and hopefully it would not be long before he was back. With deep sincerity, I

Eventually a sodden, dark apparition appeared.

thanked him for his help and he went on his way. It was now a question of waiting for Derek to return. Still with the heating turned up high, I was more than happy waiting in the car although I felt guilty at having let down the ladies' group, who by now would have realised that we weren't going to make it.

The longer I sat there the more I started to think that perhaps I ought to drive to meet Derek coming back. But then what if he had met someone he knew, who then gave him a lift back and the car would not be where he was expecting it to be? No, I decided, it was better to stay put and wait. Eventually a sodden, dark apparition appeared in the distance as Derek squelched his way back to me, surprised to find me in a car with the engine running. As he sat back in his seat with the rivulets of water running down his forehead, I explained what had happened.

'Well, we're still going to have to stay here,' he snapped, 'because Sam is on his way now and he will expect us to be here.'

'At least', I soothed, 'you will have the chance to warm up with the engine running.'

'And the mechanic got it going, just like that you say', Derek complained bitterly.

'Well – yes – but then he is a mechanic, and it was only because I was on my own that he was able to do it', I tried to reason.

'Did he say anything else?' Derek asked.

'Just one thing', I replied, pointing at a light in the near distance through the back window. 'You see that light down the road?'

'Yes', said Derek, turning his head to look.

'He said it is a garage with a phone outside!' We waited for Sam in silence!

Carey the badger and her three cubs were still doing well, although I was slightly concerned over the size of the cubs who were much smaller than the ones being hand-reared in the kitchen. There had been some concern over whether Carey would have enough milk for them all. Having chatted to Liz, our vet, we decided that we needed to blood-test the mother as part of the health protocol that the badgers go through. So when we anaesthetised the sow, it would give us the opportunity to check the cubs over while she was asleep and find out their sex.

Liz arrived complete with her black box and we strolled down to the casualty pens.

'Busy today', Liz said, as we passed an excited school party filing in with their picnic boxes.

'Yes,' I replied, 'and it's nice to have a sunny day – they always enjoy themselves more if the sun's shining.'

Opening the metal door to the pens we ducked under the top door and peered through the window of the door of the pen where Carey and her three cubs were.

'Well, they've certainly grown since I saw them last,' Liz said, 'but I can see what you mean in comparison with the cubs in the kitchen.'

Opening her box, Liz got out the sedation drug and drew the injection from the bottle. I had a thick blanket with me, and opening the door, I went in and quietly covered Carey and the three cubs with the blanket. Turning back the cover so that the sow's rump was exposed, I kept my hand over where her head was to be aware of any movement on her part.

'OK', I nodded to Liz. She quickly came in and confidently injected her. Pulling the blanket off carefully as we left the pen, we shut the door to allow the drug to work.

'That was easy', remarked Liz.

'She's been so good, all the way through. Even having to inject her each day when she arrived, once she knew what we were doing, she's been no trouble at all', I said.

We both leant over the door. Carey rested her head on her paws – already she was beginning to feel sleepy.

'What's going to happen to her?' Liz asked.

'Well,' I replied, 'you know she was found locally in a shed that has since been pulled down; but there are other sheds there, so I did think that once the cubs are weaned we could put them all in a shed for a while and then after a couple of weeks, just leave the door open. After all, it would be the territory where she came from. But having discussed it with Colin from West Hatch, taking into account that she did have territorial wounds and is quite an old badger, it seems a shame to put her back into an area where she may have to fight to survive. So we have decided to mix her with some other cubs, if all goes well, and release them as a family unit in a new release site where there will be no other badgers. This will give time for her family to settle in and offer the best chance of survival for them all. She deserves that at the very least, bless her.'

'I think she should be out now', said Liz. So carefully I went in, picked up Carey and carried her through to the examination room so that Liz could take blood. Even though the badger was sedated, Liz placed a muzzle over the mouth for safety and then gave her a complete check-over. Her wounds had healed completely and she was now in very good condition. Taking the blood from the jugular vein, Liz's job was soon done.

Leaving Carey quietly snoozing, we went back into the pen to look at the cubs. Despite looking small, on inspection they were all quite chunky and were obviously getting enough milk to get by on. So happily, it was not going to be necessary to take one away to allow for more milk for the others, as we thought we might have to. The cubs were two females and a male. Very spitty and indignant cubs, not at all used to being disturbed, let alone handled.

'Great,' enthused Liz, 'they're fine. Now all we need to do is reverse the anaesthetic and put Mum back.'

Soon the family were back together again – Mum a little bit sleepy, but three cubs pleased to have that warm, musky body to hide under. Then three small black and white heads surfaced again, two between her paws and a third by her belly. If ever there was a picture of contentment – that was it. All was well.

Meadow

Meadow was the next cub to join the kitchen crew and he was to be the most difficult feeder ever. He was found starving up above ground and one can only assume that either his mother had been killed or he had come up above ground with her, lost contact and wandered so far from home that she had not found him again.

Badger cubs are sometimes still suckling when they are 8 to 9 weeks old and are unable to survive if they have not made the change on to solid food. Because, in comparison to puppies, they appear self-sufficient, we have even known badger cubs to die under veterinary care where they were left with saucers of food which, of course, they showed no interest in.

Meadow had been without food for quite some time and his long fur belied the scrawny body underneath. Consequently, when offered a bottle of milk, he would latch on to the teat and clamp his jaws rigid so that it was impossible to pull the teat out of his mouth. Because the teat was flattened the milk did not flow through, and a very frightened little cub was desperately worried that the attempts to pull the teat out of his mouth to allow the air in so that the milk would come through, were really attempts to deprive him of the food that he had at last found.

It was a question of being patient and sitting with him, allowing him time to relax and to cajole him into letting you, at the very least, just move the teat from side to side so that the air could bubble through the milk in the bottle and so allow him to feed. It is not easy, especially when there are another three cubs scrambling up your legs because they have smelt the milk and want their share, which in turn activated Barley and Ebony who were now living in the cubby-hole, and were sure it was time for their food also. Barley still had that endearing quality of crying pitifully once he wanted his food until it arrived.

At these times, Derek would always suddenly remember something he had to do and I would be left with the wailing group of starving cubs. Meadow continued to be a very difficult feeder for several days and at times would have tried the patience of a saint! One session, when it had taken over an hour to get a feed down him, the entry on his record sheet said 'nearly had his neck wrung'! Eventually, we got into a routine that worked, although this had its hiccups at times as Glade, Flora and Poppy were now dropping a feed and starting solids.

Bottle-feeding can be hard work but the real fun is when the cubs start to eat solid food. Not being keen on regurgitating earthworms, as we are given to believe sow badgers do for their

73

cubs, I usually start them with baby foods. But of course, unused to bowls, the cubs first snorkel in the food and then delight in scooping all the contents on to the newspaper so carefully laid to catch all the mess. The next stage is to spread it around the floor until they have a pile of food on the end of their noses, and then they blow down their noses to see how far up the walls they can get it. This may not be quite the truth, but it certainly appears to be the results of their endeavours.

It is amazing how clean your kitchen can be when you wash the floor, walls and all unit surfaces at least three times a day. Who said that animals in the kitchen are unhealthy?

Glade and Poppy decided to do some cleaning themselves one day when they mastered the art of opening the drawers to the kitchen cabinet. Lying on their backs and getting the claws of their front paws just under the edge of the drawer, they discovered that the drawer would slide open. What's more, by climbing into this drawer Glade discovered that he could then open the next drawer, and so on like a ladder until he was able to achieve the dizzy heights of the top of the sink unit.

Most of the dirty dishes, thankfully, were in the sink, but the dishcloth was draped over the side dripping water on to the floor. An attempt on the red knob of the washing-up liquid bottle led to it falling on its side so that it slowly rolled along the

. . . they discovered that the drawer would slide open.

surface and on to the floor. The impact was enough to split the plastic sides of the bottle and the green soapy liquid oozed slowly over the floor. This somewhat added to the sliding capabilities of the quarry tiled floor and Poppy and Flora, whilst trying to catch the rolling bottle, slipped and slithered their way around. Glade, obviously wanting a piece of the action, only made it back down to the second drawer until his way was blocked, so he amused himself by evicting the contents of the cleaning drawer – from cloths and brushes to polish tins and scouring pads. He then amazed himself by biting the tube of brass cleaner which, with a little bit of pressure, caused the creamy paste to spiral out in jets like spaghetti over everything else remaining in the drawer. Meadow, one can only assume, felt he had not been in the fold long enough to help make such a mess and slept quietly behind the armchair while this was all going on.

You know how you come into a room and as you smell cleaning materials your first thought is that someone has been thoroughly cleaning? My split-second dream was very quickly dispelled as I opened the kitchen door and my eyes slowly reached the floor. Two green little horrors with spiked-up fur scrabbled towards the chair having been discovered, but their attempts at speed merely led to their back legs sliding to one side as they were propelled through the washing-up liquid on their bellies. White bubbly spittle foamed from their mouths from playing with the split bottle. Glade, with chains of yellow paste draped over each ear, strained just too far over the side of the drawer and fell straight into the green puddle below. A third spiky horror – only this one was green and yellow – attempted a dash towards the chair.

Scooping all three up together before their attempts at reaching the chair succeeded in causing even more mess to be cleared up, I dumped all three in our big bath and fixed the hair spray to the taps. I have never seen so many suds in my life and it was absolutely ages before the water ran clear. I'm not sure if the shine on their coats came from the soap or the brass cleaner, but a cleaner set of cubs would have been hard to find once they were all towelled dry. The next bit of fun was the floor – the drawers – the unit – the chair legs – the kitchen rug . . .

You must really miss them when they go, people say to me time and time again – yes, really, really, really!

5

The Strawberry Blond

The ringing of the telephone jarred my deep sleep, as I floundered to turn on the bedside light. Squinting at the bright light, my next move was to lift the receiver, and irrespective of the time and of my still being half asleep, the usual 'Good evening, Secret World' tripped off my tongue. Pulling up to a sitting position I looked at the other side of the bed, which was empty, and glanced at the clock: 1.30 a.m. and Derek was still not home from a boys' night out with the cricket team.

All sorts of things race through my mind until I catch the word 'RSPCA' and realise that it is a night call-out and not a taxi request from Derek, or the police telling me something was wrong.

'Sorry,' I mumbled, 'can you start that again, you've got my full attention now.'

Sliding the notepad over towards me, I picked up the pen to write down notes. A lady had discovered a badger in her garden that appeared to be having fits. She had reported it to the RSPCA, but they did not have an Inspector in the area and I was being asked to respond to the call-out. Taking directions, name and telephone numbers, it was only a matter of minutes before I had my clothes pulled on and was on my way downstairs.

I was to meet the midnight (or early morning!) reveller on the stairs on the way to bed. The giggle as we met was all I needed to know that it was just as well if I went on my own. With 'See you when I get home', the ships passed each other.

Using a torch to find my way to the new casualty pens, I collected the cage and equipment and decided to put it in the 'runaround' car that we had just purchased from the local car auction. Some of the things that we collect at times can be rather smelly and prone to go to toilet during transportation, and so we had acquired an older hatchback vehicle to use in these situations. We had only had it a week and, as yet, I had not driven it. Not mechanically minded myself, I could only tell you that it was white with four wheels. As long as it went when the key was turned in the ignition, that was all I needed to know.

I then telephoned the lady concerned to let her know I was on my way and would be with her in twenty minutes. The badger was still in her garden and she was going to monitor it until I got there.

I had to pick up the Minehead road, which is not one that I travel very often, but I knew that the village of Cannington now had a by-pass so I mentally made a note that when I got to the roundabout, which was just out of town, I had to take the second turning (which led to the village) and miss the by-pass.

Driving through the town at 2 a.m., as you can imagine, was very quiet and I was making good time. Just as I passed the last set of traffic lights in the town I came up behind a car moving at only 30 miles an hour. I presumed it was someone who perhaps had had a drink and was making sure that he wasn't going to get stopped. We were in a 40-mile-an-hour limit and soon I could see a clear part of the road ahead, so increasing speed I overtook and speeded up to 50 miles an hour.

It was soon afterwards that I noticed a blue light flashing behind me just as I came up to the roundabout. Thinking I had arrived at the Cannington roundabout, I took the second turning and by this time realised that the blue light was definitely following me, so I slowly pulled into the roadside and stopped.

Looking through my rear view mirror, I watched the police officers get out of the car and put their caps on, and at the same time assessed my surroundings. I was not at Cannington, I was driving into a housing estate. Unbeknown to me, since I had last used this road, a new roundabout had been constructed to give easier access to the houses.

The inevitable 'Good morning!' was uttered by the officer as I wound down my window. He stood by my door as the other officer walked around the car.

'Name?' was the next question.

'Pauline Kidner', I replied with a smile.

'Do you have any means of identification?' the officer asked.

I couldn't even remember if I'd combed my hair; I certainly had not thought to bring any personal possessions. 'I'm on an RSPCA call-out to an injured badger, officer, an emergency call – I didn't think to bring anything with me', I replied.

He moved to the front of the car and said, looking back at me, 'and what is your registration number?'

Feeling even more uncomfortable, I explained that I hadn't got a clue, we had only just purchased the car and . . .

'And where are you going?' His face gave no clue as to his feelings.

The inevitable 'Good morning!' was uttered by the officer . . .

'I'm going to Cannington', I replied.

'Then why did you turn up here?' he asked.

'Well, I thought I was at Cannington because this roundabout wasn't here before and I thought I was missing the by-pass.'

'You weren't trying to get away from us – you realised we were chasing you?' he questioned.

'Well, I did in the end, but I didn't know why . . .'

'Because,' he said, leaning into the car, 'you were going over 50 miles an hour in a 40 mile limit.'

'Oh, I'm so sorry, I was in a rush as the badger is fitting and the road was clear and . . .' I excused my sins.

'That', the officer solemnly stated, 'is no excuse for speeding.'

'Look, I've got all the equipment in the back, I truly am going out to a badger and I really am very sorry to have been speeding', I tried to reason.

The other officer came up behind the one standing by the car door. 'She's alright', he said, nodding his head towards me. He either knew or had heard of me. 'She's the only person I know who would be mad enough to go out at this time of night just for a badger.'

'Alright then', said the policeman who had been asking the questions, flipping over his notepad and returning it to his pocket. 'Injured badger or not, it's no excuse for speeding – go on – go and find your badger.'

I fervently thanked him and turned the ignition. Hopefully, as well as getting away with the speeding, I had not been too delayed in my journey. Eventually turning into the isolated road leading towards the power station, I took all the left and right turns described in my notes to arrive at a house with its outside lights blazing in the night.

Relieved at my arrival, the lady came out with a friend. They had been watching the badger who was still standing by the stone wall on the patio near the house. Taking the equipment through the house, I could see as we came out into the garden that the badger had its body arched and was drooling. It appeared very uncomfortable and almost oblivious of what was going on around it. From that point of view, it made the capture fairly simple. By quickly throwing a blanket over her, I was able to scoop her up into the cage.

The lady of the house was seriously worried that the badger had been poisoned and was concerned that there may be other badgers similarly in a bad condition near the sett. She explained that the sett was not that far away. You could get to it by crawling under her Leylandii hedge and through the next field.

It's not until you find that you are one of three women, on hands and knees crawling through a hedge (I have to say, it was not as simple as she had made it sound), and then tramping through a very neglected overgrown field, that you start to realise that the looks of ridicule so apparent on the policemen's faces could be warranted. Still, luckily there were no other badgers in sight, and the lady's mind was put at rest as to the thought of others suffering.

The thought of the return journey through the hedge again was not all that appealing, but eventually we were back at the house. Giving her my details, I was keen to get away so that I could get to the vet as quickly as possible. Ringing in on my mobile phone, I was able to let the on-duty vet know that I was on my way so that by the time I arrived at the veterinary hospital, Ngaire, the attending vet, was already there waiting.

Despite the hour, which was gone 3 a.m. by then, Ngaire gave the badger a complete check-over. She was very concerned at how quiet her lungs were and decided that an x-ray was needed. Working with the night nurse, the x-rays were soon taken and the seriousness of the situation became very apparent. The badger, which was a sow, had probably been involved in a car accident. The impact had punctured the wall of her lungs and part of her intestines had been pushed through, causing severe breathing difficulties. There was a need for immediate surgery with complications likely regarding infection. Despite a poor prognosis, we had to give it a try.

Not for a minute thinking that this was 'only a badger', Ngaire and the nurse moved straight into action. I left the badger in their safe care, knowing that she was about to be given an operation that was going to take at least an hour, but I also knew, as with all the work carried out at our veterinary practice, that everything possible would be done for her.

The sleeping reveller did not stir when I returned to bed, and I think that the badger was probably feeling better than Derek the next morning! When I rang to find out how she was, the nurse reported that she had recovered from the operation and would be able to come to us by the afternoon.

When we collected her, we were warned that she was not 'out

of the woods' yet. It was to be quite a long recuperation and we may still lose her at any time. The lady who reported her to us came and visited her badger a few days later and was pleased to see her comfortable in one of the casualty pens.

I wish I could say that the sow recovered and was finally released, but unfortunately, despite everybody's tremendous efforts, the badger died suddenly nearly two weeks later. Was it a waste of time, doing everything that we did – the time, the effort, the cost? Not a bit of it. Why devalue what we do, when it could so easily have had a different result. Isn't it more worrying to think of the hundreds, even thousands, of badgers injured in car accidents that die a slow death, because they aren't found or the people who see them just don't care? With 50,000 badgers killed on our roads every year, many, many more that are injured must suffer tremendously.

It was getting towards the end of April and all the badger cubs in the kitchen were doing well. Taffy, Barley and Ebony had joined the rest of the kitchen crew and were able to enjoy the rough and tumble games despite being the smallest of the group. Meadow, thank goodness, was down to only two feeds a day, but Glade, Flora and Poppy were now fully weaned and it was time for them to go down to the RSPCA grassed enclosures. Once they are able to look after themselves, it is important to move the cubs away from human contact, and certainly away from their original carer, to help them revert to being wild.

I telephoned Colin to see when they could take them and he suggested that the next Tuesday would fit in with them. It would be wrong to say that I don't feel sad when I know that they are going. After all, I had been with them since they arrived at our Centre. Each cub always has a different personality and you do become very fond of them. Glade was extra special as he had come in as the first cub after Bluebell died, but he, more than anyone, needed to go as he seemed to have a special relationship with me, which was not good.

Glade, Poppy and Flora were now at the age where they were bonding to form a group. On waking and coming up to me, the action was for the cubs to back on to my feet and scent-mark my shoes. This, in badger language, is a greeting, a way of showing that I was part of their social group, and the constant scent-marking with each other makes the smell that is individual to each family group. It was a thing that Bluebell would do, making the lovely 'uuuv vuv vuv' sound which is like a deep purr, to say hello. My shoes, as far as another badger was concerned, must have stunk of badger! I was therefore aware that it was time for these cubs to move on before the trust in humans became impossible to change.

The next day I received a telephone call that started with 'Hi, Pauline, this is Mike Gunton – remember me?'

'How', I teased, 'could I possibly forget a strawberry blond!'

The film crew wanted to do some footage of the cubs in the kitchen and then to follow them down to the RSPCA. So it was arranged that they would be with us early Tuesday morning to film them prior to moving down to the RSPCA. We had also decided to make our own video of what goes on at our crazy home, so there was a friend called Jason Venus, better known for his fantastic photographs, also with us on the day to film the film crew filming me – if you get what I mean!

As far as the badger cubs were concerned, it was wonderful. Plenty of new bags, equipment, fluffy microphone covers and different people invading the kitchen meant that the last thing the cubs were going to do was act naturally with so many other things going on!

Cameras attempted to take footage of the cubs on the kitchen floor, only to have a cub walk straight up to the lens and deposit a very wet nose on the glass or walk straight past the camera to investigate this new person lying on the floor. Even if the cameraman did manage to get some film of one badger playing, it was at the expense of having another cub nibbling his ear while he tried to hold the camera steady.

Glade was in his element in all this. A true leader of the pack, he was very bolshie. As soon as he was placed on the kitchen floor in front of the armchair, with a view to filming him climbing on to me with all the other cubs, he would scoot around the back of the film crew and charge around causing havoc. As soon as a hand was put down, he would roll over on his back, grab the sleeve (which usually involved part of the arm as well) and grip with his feet. Even at this age, their teeth can be quite sharp!

'The sooner he goes the better', I said. 'He's too brave for his own good.'

Luckily, all the crew had a good sense of humour and they eventually got the kind of shots they were looking for. There was panic for a short while when Meadow appeared to have gone missing, only for him to be found sound asleep in one of the equipment bags!

All too soon, it was time to put the older cubs into a cage and start the journey down to West Hatch. As I placed the cage on the back seat of the car and covered it with a blanket, the cubs whickered at their strange surroundings. I knew they would eventually settle but felt guilty at upsetting them. With the film crew following behind, we set off to the RSPCA.

The film crew wanted to follow the whole process of the protocol that our cubs go through, so as soon as we arrived, I explained to the cameras that the cubs would be taken to the consultancy and operation room where we would first weigh each cub to find out the correct dosage for anaesthesia and then check their microchip numbers using a scanner.

Handling the cubs had to be done with care. Taken out of the kitchen environment and scared, they were just as likely, in all the confusion, to nip as a wild one would. Injected by the resident RSPCA vet, each cub, once it had become sleepy, was placed on the table. Using a hand-held scanner, the vet checked over the neck area of the cub to find the identichip that had been given to each cub as soon as it was taken into captivity. The scanner screen shows the individual number of the identichip.

We keep record sheets for each individual animal that comes into care and a copy of the sheet for each cub would be taken down to the RSPCA. This will tell them when the cubs came in to us, their log number, identichip number and whether they are male or female. It will tell them about any medical condition they may have had, and also detail any drugs or treatment they have received as well as giving the result of their first blood test. Their age, weight gains and feeding times, as well as food content, will all be detailed on these sheets as a very comprehensive record of what has happened to this cub during its time with us.

The cameras continued to roll as the vet clipped the fur from the leg of each cub so that they could take a blood sample. I explained to the cameras that because of a disease called bovine TB which badgers can occasionally carry, we follow a health regime of blood-testing each animal three times during their period of captivity in order to be as responsible as possible in making sure that only healthy animals are released back to the wild.

In fact, we categorise cubs when they are found. If they come from an area where there has been TB in the cattle, then these are reared by Gill Pearce in Cornwall. Those cubs, eventually grouped, will only be released in the South-West. If the cubs are found in areas clear of bovine TB, then they will come to us and, subject to the same three-test condition, will be released in other parts of the country. With so many misconceptions on the TB issue, which has raged for over twenty years, it is better to follow a protocol accepted by the Ministry of Agriculture, Fisheries and Food, than to blindly release animals with no health regime at all, even if you do not believe that badgers are the culprit in this ongoing saga.

Once the cub has been blood-tested, it goes into the next room where Colin Seddon is ready to tattoo each cub in turn. The cub is laid on its back. Using a trimmer, Colin carefully shaves the hair from the inside of each back leg and the same numbers are tattooed on each side.

Glade, being the first cub to be brought in that year, would be number 1 followed by the last two digits of the year. This gives each cub a visual number that will stay with them for the rest of their lives. People would rarely think of checking a dead badger for an identichip number. But if the animal is examined, it would be hard to miss the large lettering on the legs and it is hoped that people would think to report them either to the police or the RSPCA.

One of the biggest problems with all wildlife is knowing the success of the ones that you are able to release. Putting rings on birds or tattooing animals means that you can assess whether what you are doing is allowing an animal to survive. Only this year a badger was killed on a road and, because of the tattoo, was reported to the police. It was sad in a way because, from the number, we knew it was a female that had been released as a cub three years earlier. But the good part was that she was in excellent condition, so prior to her death, she had survived well and had successfully integrated into the wild.

All too often, proper fieldwork and careful consideration of a release site can be lacking, and a release is read as a success, just because the animals or birds walk or fly off into the distance. I suspect that on many occasions the opposite is nearer the truth.

'How are the sow and cubs doing?' Colin asked.

'Really well', I answered. 'The cubs have not grown as quickly as our hand-reared ones but then "our lot" probably get more food than they would in the wild, so it's hardly surprising. Liz came out and checked them when she blood-tested the sow and they look fine. Her cubs are eating solids now and catching up fast so I thought that when you have another three orphan cubs ready to come to us, I would integrate them with her to form a group of seven.'

'That's great', he replied. 'I've got a really super release site for her.'

I smiled at him. Colin had been out and taken photographs of the sow and cubs and I truly think she had touched his heart. Always a matter-of-fact type of person, he rarely shows emotion, but his attachment to her was obvious.

Once the badgers had been tattooed, they were taken down to the pens in the isolation unit to recover from their anaesthetic. Slowly each one came round and I spent time with them, trying to console them in their strange environment. Three other badgers had been through the same procedure and were being added to them; these were ones that were already weaned when they had arrived at the RSPCA and they had been kept at the unit. Having three wild ones put with Glade, Flora and Poppy would help them adjust to their new surroundings with wild instincts of caution.

At last it was time to say goodbye. It seemed so difficult, especially with Glade. In a way he had supported me through the loss of Bluebell and the hours we had shared together while he had been a single cub had brought back so many memories of time with Blue. He whimpered with the effects of the anaesthetic and from fear of the new surroundings. Close to tears, I stroked them for the last time. As I got up, Glade, Poppy and Flora followed me to the door, worried that I was going to leave them behind – which was exactly what I was going to do. Pushing them back inside the pen, I closed the door and left them to become a new family in a fresh home. I didn't look back as I walked away – I couldn't.

The next day, with all the effects of the anaesthetic gone, all six cubs would go into a large grassed enclosure with an artificial sett. Surprisingly, they will quickly revert to being nocturnal. They will be able to do proper badgery things such as rooting for insects, foraging for earthworms on the specially mown areas, and playing chase through the long grass with their new friends. I doubt they will give their old home another thought.

Going back to the kitchen at home, with only four cubs left, it seems a quieter place. Sensing my mood, Meadow, Taffy, Barley and Ebony all climbed on to my lap and snuggled up together. I allowed myself twenty minutes to enjoy their company while I had a cup of coffee before getting up to go out to the orchard.

Francis Farr-Cox was due to arrive any minute, with fresh plants for the dipping pond. Francis has been a regular visitor to our Centre for many years with his wife Tricia and son Phillip. He has the dubious honour of being known locally as 'spider-man'. This does not mean that he runs around wearing a red mask and blue tights, just that he is an invertebrate specialist with a particular interest in spiders!

In fact, on our Creepy Crawlie Weekends, Francis, as our resident Field Detective, looks far more impressive with his outdoor clothes and range of nets for pond-dipping and hedge-sweeping. He always wears a body warmer with thousands of pockets carrying magnifying glasses, tiny jars, pipettes, tweezers and, of course, a tuning fork. Why a tuning fork, you may ask? Well, you knock it on a solid object to make it vibrate and then hold it gently to a spider's web. The vibration on the web tricks the spider into thinking he has caught some prey and he dashes out to catch it. This sadistic act of deception enables Francis to identify the spider to the audience – though it is very disappointing to the spider! Actually, once you get into the world of bugs and beetles it is really fascinating. There are many different kinds of web spun by spiders; there is even a spitting spider who, instead of spinning a web and waiting for it to trap their prey, actually identify their victim and then immobilise them by spitting a jet of silk to cover them.

Together with Francis, we had decided to create a dipping pond as our duck pond was far too deep and its levels varied according to the amount of rain that fell in a season. The Environment Agency gave us a grant and Francis was the main man as far as the organisation and design of the pond were concerned. It turned out to be a running nightmare!

The heavy machinery was ordered to come and dig the large hole ready for the pond, and there had been great ideas of where all the excess earth was going to go. We had many dips in our car park and several gulleys in the homeground that needed filling in,

GLADE - MY NEW BEGINNING

"THE KITCHEN CREW"

A TEN-WEEK-OLD BLACK AND WHITE BUNDLE

WE JUST LOVE PEANUT BUTTER!

I'M SIZE TEN - HOW ABOUT YOU?

TEDDY FOR COMPANY

A QUIET SNOOZE

O SMALL, TAFFY WAS FED ON A SYRINGE

Jason Venus

DEBBIE OUT COLLECTING A CASUALTY

Author

DEREK, MORE BUSINESSMAN THAN FARMER THESE DAYS

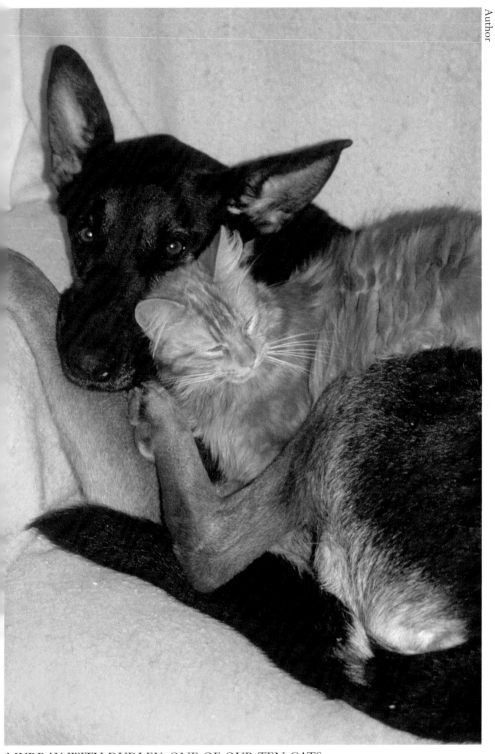

Author

MURRAY WITH DUDLEY, ONE OF OUR TEN CATS

WILMA THE WEASEL NEEDING A HELPING HAND

SO SMALL THEY CAN FIT INTO A BIRD BOX

A BROWN DISC UNDER THE CHIN - I'M A WEASE

CAREY AND HER THREE TINY CUBS

Mike Hollist

Gary Sealey

PAULINE WITH GORDON, SO
SADLY MISSED BY ALL

SARAH WITH ONE OF HER
'FOXY FRIENDS'

so it was all going to be so easy. As with all these things, two weeks prior to work commencing it decided to rain continuously so that by the time the day came the ground was just ripe to be churned up, far too wet to move the soil – so we ended up with little mountains all over the place and the once green and attractive orchard soon looked like a demolition site.

At the end of the day, Francis, myself, Derek and the workmen surveyed the area, each agreeing that a bit of fine weather would soon put it all right. I don't think anyone was feeling particularly confident at this point. But time is a great healer and as it dried and the soil was moved about, we were soon ready for the next phase of lining the pond with sand and the liner to be put in place. Sandbags were placed around the edge to protect the liner, and extra soil was added around the perimeter for the emergent plants to grow. We were unaware that we were being watched. With just a few plants placed around the pond, it was beginning to look attractive and it was easy to see how, once the plants had taken root, it would soon become a haven for wildlife.

The next morning, as Derek walked through the orchard, he was to see that, indeed, the 'wildlife' had started to move in. Proudly dabbling in the centre of the new dipping pond were three Muscovy ducks from our duck pond. This was particularly worrying as they have very long claws on their webbed feet and we were concerned for the safety of the liner. Each hour it got worse, and despite our frantic efforts of shouting, waving sticks and even throwing things at the ducks, more and more 'wildlife' moved from the duck pond to the new dipping pond. By the time Francis called in the afternoon to survey his previous day's work, the duck pond was almost empty and the dipping pond was full of ducks and three geese with the last shreds of the new pond weed trailing from their beaks.

With the aid of a large net, we eventually evicted the unwanted ducks from the new pond. This net had to remain draped over the pond until new higher fencing, backed with chicken wire, was erected. We then had to cover the entire pond with a net large enough for people to get in under but that would still discourage the ducks! Eventually, after all the contingency plans and a couple of determined ducks ending up in the deep freeze, the problem was sorted, new plants added and the pond began to blossom.

In fact, last summer it all looked so attractive on a very hot day that our eldest son, Barry, now in his late twenties, who was

Derek discovered them and was absolutely fuming . . .

staying with us for a couple of days, decided with his cousin to go into the pond for a swim! Derek discovered them and was absolutely fuming after all the work that had gone into creating this dipping pond – the time and cost of fencing and netting and now – here were two lads larking around in his precious pond.

Barry laughed in the kitchen as he towelled his hair dry and regaled the event to me.

'Gosh,' he said, 'I haven't seen Dad jump up and down, shaking his fists and shouting like that for a long time. He was so cross – it was just like being a kid again!'

Francis had brought some fresh species for the pond which was now beginning to teem with life. In just two years the proliferation of species was amazing: newts had moved in and the occasional grass snake would be seen swimming across.

'It's very established now, isn't it', Francis said as he admired the surface of the water.

'Took a bit of time,' he added wryly, 'but it was worth it.'

'Well worth all the effort, and particularly yours, you worked very hard', I commented.

Sarah, our Animal Supervisor, called out to me that a casualty had arrived.

'You go on,' said Francis, 'I'm just going to put these plants in and I shall be gone. See you soon.'

I thanked him and turned to go into the hospital room where a family had just arrived having driven all the way from Wales. Mrs Wakelan had telephoned the previous evening to explain that they had found a small baby animal on a golf course and were not sure what it was. Having taken it to a vet, they had been told that it was probably a lurcher puppy, but she was wondering if it was a badger cub. She described it to me as grey in colour and, although not having a striped black and white face, it had two lighter patches at the top of its head.

'Is that what I can hear whining in the background?' I asked.

'Yes,' she replied, 'we have been feeding it but it does seem to whine a lot.'

'I think,' I said, 'if you look at the end of its tail you will find a white tip – it sounds to me very much like a fox cub.'

She confirmed that it had the white tip and asked if we would be prepared to rear it. They had done a very good job so far, but realising the commitment and the need for correct rearing, they were prepared to bring it over to us. We have had fox cubs mistaken for puppies and kittens before as people very rarely realise that they vary in colour from grey to chocolate brown when they are very tiny, and the patches on the head are the red fur starting to come through.

The family were already in the hospital room when I arrived, with Sarah taking their details. The children were fascinated by the array of animals in tubs and cages being cared for. Although the public are not allowed into this room, it is sometimes good, especially for children, to see the need for care for injured and orphaned wildlife. Whilst upset at not being able to keep the fox cub, the children could see that it was going to be well cared for and we promised to send them details of how the cub progressed.

The fox cub was only 7 to 10 days old and the family had quite rightly left the cub for as long as possible in the hope of the mother returning. But being so small it was soon getting cold and needed to be taken care of. It is a fine line with all orphans, as sometimes action taken too quickly can mean that babies are taken into care when it is not necessary, but once they show signs of stress or discomfort, then they must be looked after.

Sarah does most of the fox cub rearing for us. She has always had an interest in foxes. We try to encourage staff to take responsibility for baby animals as the young ones will always do much better with one main carer looking after them all the time.

Even with their eyes closed, wildlife babies pick up on scent and on routines of feeding and caring, and they will respond much better to one person alone.

The little fox cub was taken out of the box and the children patiently explained about the feeds that it had been given and how it had been looked after. Mrs Wakelan had even, very sensibly, brought the milk that the cub was being fed on and the teat that he had got used to. This would all make the transition to a new carer much easier for the cub. Sarah assured them that she would take great care of the fox and, with a few tears, the children left with their parents for their return journey.

Woody, as the little fox cub had been named, was wrapped in a towel, content in the crook of Sarah's arm.

'Start of the sleepless nights, Sarah!' I teased.

'I know,' she said, 'but he's lovely and I don't mind doing it.' She would indeed look after him very well, not counting all the extra time after work that she would have to put in, and feeds through the night as well. I am sure we have put many of our girls off the idea of having a baby once they realise that feeds still have to be done even if you're tired when you come home from an evening out and then it's up again early the next morning – even on your day off!

I also can get exhausted by it all and was very pleased when Debbie offered one evening, when she was on a late duty, to stay on and do a midnight feed for Taffy and Ebony so that I could have an early night. The thought was very tempting and I accepted. It was the Saturday night of the Spring Bank Holiday. Derek was out again – I don't want you to think this is a regular thing (!) but it always seems that if anything is going to happen, then it will be when Derek is missing.

It was great. I curled up in bed with a book and it was not long before I began to feel sleepy. Switching off the light at around ten o'clock, I was soon dead to the world. Debbie finished all her chores and fed the badger cubs before finally checking on the hospital room and dropping the latch on the door as she made her way home.

Sweet dreams were all too soon interrupted by the telephone ringing. It was just before 1 a.m. and a man called Michael Manchip, who lived in the nearby town of Weston-super-Mare, was ringing with a badger problem. A week ago, when he had passed by a small piece of scrubland, he had seen a dead badger on the side of the road. Michael hadn't thought much of it other than being surprised that badgers were still in the vicinity. All around there was a new housing development and only this small area remained overgrown. There had been quite a large sett in there at one time but this had become disused with all the disturbance, and it had become a children's play area with dens made out of old bits of wood and with rubbish everywhere.

Michael had a certain amount of knowledge of badgers and on his way home from the pub had decided to have a look by the old sett to see if there were any signs of use. As he arrived at the sett, he saw very small and pathetically thin badger cubs scurry back down the hole. He had remained nearby and could hear their plaintive cries underground. He then realised that the dead badger could well have been a lactating sow, and these poor little cubs had been without food for over a week.

He did not know what to do. Taking the details, I arranged to meet him in a road near the piece of scrubland. Pulling on my clothes (so much for the early night!), I gathered up cages, grasper, hot water bottles and blankets as well as a torch. Leaving a note to Derek, explaining where I had gone, I was soon on my way.

By the time I reached Weston, it was gone 1 a.m. and most of the streets were empty. Certainly, once I reached the housing estate, nearly all the house lights were off. I waited in the arranged place and Michael soon arrived. He was tall and in his late twenties, and was very concerned for the welfare of the cubs. He blamed himself for not thinking to look at the sow when he had seen her dead on the road because he would have seen if she had been lactating. Hindsight is a wonderful thing, and it's so easy to think we could have done something different – but the very fact that he was here in the middle of the night trying to do something about the situation was more than most people would be prepared to do.

We made our way to the sett. Not being children, it was not easy either to scale the wall, or to make our way along the network of tunnels through the undergrowth covering very uneven ground. Eventually reaching a clearing in the centre, I could distinctly hear the cries of the cubs. We put down the cages and equipment and sat close to the entrance, listening. It was going to be a case of sitting and waiting and hoping that they would come up to the surface. There seemed little point in both of us staying and so Michael went home, promising to come up early in the morning to see if the cubs were still there.

I settled near to the sett entrance. The blankets brought for the cubs were welcome as it was quite a cold night, and I sat on one and pulled the other one around my shoulders. The cries were whimpers as they sounded sleepy, and then all was quiet as if they had indeed gone to sleep, but within ten minutes the cries would start again. Sometimes it sounded stronger as if they were coming near to the surface but then they would fade away again. I had heard enough cries from cubs to know that they sounded very weak.

It is so frustrating sitting by a sett in that type of situation. Legally, you are not allowed to interfere with a sett and it may be that you have read the whole situation wrongly and there is not a problem. Other badgers may be underground, although I very much doubted this as it all seemed disused. It was a Bank Holiday so no licensing bodies would be available until Tuesday – two, nearly three, days away. That would be too late for these cubs.

Despite the discomfort of briars and hard ground I dozed in the silent times but was soon roused by the cries once they started again. You start to wonder why you're there in such a hopeless situation. Just what am I doing sitting on my own in a bit of scrubland in the middle of the night? Well, I reason with myself, hardly any rapists are going to go mooching around here for a victim, are they? And anyway, the whole place is surrounded by houses – if anything happened, people would hear my screams. With that comforting thought, I continued to sit. I watched as sensor lights attached to several houses came on as probably a fox, or even a badger, made their way through the gardens in search of food – or it could even be a cat, I considered.

All of a sudden a man could be heard shouting at the top of his voice. This was followed by the lights going on in one house and a woman's voice screaming abuse. Doors banged and the argument raged. My God, I thought to myself, they'll wake everyone up. But not one of the other houses' lights went on nor was there any sign of anyone as this torrent of noise and scream-ing came to a crescendo; then just as quickly it stopped and all was silent again.

So much, I thought to myself, as I sat considering my position, for my ideas of any help in the event of being attacked! I was alright, just a bit longer and then I'd have to go home. My confidence was shattered as my mobile rang – I had forgotten it was in my pocket. In the quiet of the night, it sounded like Big Ben. It was Derek: having got home and read my note, he had gone to bed but had woken again and as it was now 4 a.m. he wondered where I was – such thoughtfulness!

'I'm OK', I said, explaining the situation. 'I think I'll pull out now just in case I'm stopping a sow from going back into the sett by being here, but I doubt that is the case.' The cubs were still crying but there seemed to be no movement now at all. On reaching the car, I contacted the RSPCA emergency service to explain what was going on. At that time of night all calls were going to London so we could do no more until the morning. I reluctantly returned home to grab even fewer hours than I usually got each night before I could sort anything out in the morning – so much for the early night!

Early the next morning Michael confirmed that the cubs could still be heard crying. It was therefore safe to assume that no sow had returned. I contacted emergency numbers for English Nature and MAFF, both licensing bodies, but was unable to speak to anyone other than answerphones.

I then contacted our badger group chairman, Adrian Coward, who was prepared to go out immediately and assess the situation in daylight. With feeds due again for my cubs, I was unable to go but I telephoned Linda, who is a trustee of our charity and often helps with our badgers, and she arranged to meet Michael and Adrian on site as soon as possible. Other phone calls to the RSPCA and the police had both resulted in no officers actually being able to attend but agreement that, for the welfare of the cubs, it would be best to get them to the surface as soon as possible.

Adrian is a very experienced badger consultant and was of the same opinion as myself that this old sett was being used as a breeding chamber only. With careful digging, he was able to excavate a very limited part of the sett and reach the cubs which were not too far from the surface. They were only about six weeks old, both males. One cub still had some energy as he fluffed up and spat at Adrian as he reached in to pick him up, but the other cub lost consciousness from being so scared and weak. I doubt that he would have survived for another day. Linda wrapped the two very thin little cubs in a blanket with a nice warm hot water bottle, and they were soon on their way to us.

David and Eric, and David and Eric

After veterinary check-ups and regular feeds, David and Eric, as the two cubs were named, soon became strong again. It is amazing how quickly, from being spitting, terrified young animals, the cubs can soon settle once in the kitchen environment with other cubs. If they had been weaned, there would be no need to try to get them to trust human beings, but as they still required milk feeds, it was essential for me to build up their confidence so that I could handle them. The kitchen crew were back up to six again, all as mischievous as each other. Even Murray, who was very good with them, would choose to climb up in the chair to escape them if they were all full of beans at the same time.

You may wonder why we changed from our usual countryside names for the cubs to 'David and Eric', but there was a very good reason for this. A large local grocery firm with two stores called Sanders were bought out by Tesco; one of the stores was to be closed down completely so there was a grand sale to dispose of the goods. As well as being a grocery store there was also a garden centre and, having visited with my mother in the last few weeks before the close-down, I noticed that they had a lot of green plastic netting that would be suitable for the bat cage that we were trying to build. I mentioned this to Debbie, who is the one who does all the orphan bat rearing, and suggested that she gave Tesco a ring to see if they would be prepared to donate it to us.

A few hours later Debbie was deep in conversation on the phone to David Allcock, the man in charge of winding up the store. Luckily he also had an interest in wildlife and invited Debbie over to discuss ways in which they could help us. It was through this chance phone call that we received a great deal of help from Tesco, to whom we are deeply grateful. Not only did we get our netting but also fixtures and fittings were given to us, David being bemused as to the uses to which some of these were put. If you visit our Centre, you will walk through the Bluebell Sett charity room which has displays that explain all about our work with wildlife. A section of the room has monitors showing work being carried out behind the scenes in the hospital room and casualty pens (cameras and monitors courtesy of Tesco – the security system), the room is lined with units housing stationery and information and holding up interpretation boards (units courtesy of Tesco – from the bakery section) and a large thatched roof covers part of the display (all dismantled from over the greengrocery section). We even have a large four-foot square unit with plastic sides where our harvest mice are kept in a display with ears of corn to depict a field – the unit was originally a French stick holder!

Eric Woods was also with David, assisting with the very hard job of closing the store down and disposing of all the goods, and he has continued with the support for our charity through Tesco at Weston. As well as many other ways of helping us, a special basket is kept at their branch for customers to donate food towards our many, many casualties and this has reduced our feeding costs enormously. So as a token of our gratitude for the tremendous help that has made such a difference to us, we promised to name two of our cubs after them. Hence the arrival of David and Eric, who were very happy with their names and very happy in their new home.

We were at the stage where the cubs were still having milk feeds, but at the end of the day, it was not a good idea to go to bed before first barricading the fridge door and pushing the table against the kitchen unit drawers. Both Murray and Barney had taken to sleeping in my office in order to get an undisturbed night without black and white fiends cavorting around the floor.

Even I was looking forward to a weekend break in the middle of May. The constant night feeds and attention takes its toll and I was beginning to feel very tired, but there was another reason for this planned break. Debbie had agreed to stay over in the house and look after the Centre and the cubs. Unbeknown to Derek, he and I were off to Paris!

6

Packed Suitcases

Derek was celebrating his fiftieth birthday and as a surprise, I had organised a weekend in Paris. It was to include a concert with Tina Turner, one of Derek's favourite singers, but the difficulty was how to carry out the surprise. I commandeered several of our friends to try and help with the secret.

On the Thursday night two of Derek's mates asked him out for the evening, and while he was gone from the house, it gave me time to pack his suitcase as well as my own ready for a few days away. I had already arranged for Debbie and her partner Mike to stay at our farm to oversee things; the cricket team had been told that he would not be playing that Saturday and all other normal arrangements had been cancelled.

I had booked rail tickets to London to connect with the Euro Tunnel to Paris, and the hotel and concert tickets were all part of the package. The trick was how to get Derek to the rail station without him knowing all this. I enlisted the aid of a friend called Adrian Clark, who runs a cycle hire business. He talked Derek into going to see a non-existent person in Wiltshire for a business breakfast to talk about seasonal holiday cycle hire. Adrian was to pick Derek up at 7 a.m. and drive to Bridgwater, which is about ten minutes away. Here they were to catch the 7.20 train through to London. This train stopped at Highbridge, a small town only a few miles away from us, where only a few trains stop.

In between Derek leaving the farm and reaching Bridgwater, I was to quickly dress and our son, Barry, who was staying over, was to drive me to Highbridge station. When the train pulled in at Highbridge, Adrian was to get off and I was to get on with the suitcases and the tickets to tell Derek the real reason for being on the train. Brilliant – as long as it all went to plan!

On the Thursday evening Derek got ready to go out with Robin Spooner and Ken Chapman. Just where was his best jumper, he complained, as it wasn't in the wardrobe.

'I expect it's in the washing', I replied casually.

'But it wasn't dirty', Derek argued.

'No, but it had got terribly creased so I thought it would be better for a wash – anyway, you've got plenty of other jumpers', I replied.

Satisfied with the explanation, Derek put on something else and was soon gone for his evening out. I packed the cases and tucked them away in the boys' bedrooms upstairs. All was going well.

The alarm rang at 6.30 the next morning and my cup of coffee was brought to me in bed. I didn't dare get out of bed until Derek called up to say that Adrian had arrived and he would see me later. Shouting up to Barry, I quickly dressed and in a matter of minutes we were also on the way to the railway station, but heading towards Highbridge.

The station at Highbridge is a very small one with no buildings and the train was due to arrive at 7.25. 'Here it comes!' exclaimed Barry, seeing the train coming in the distance, and we stood waiting for the small two-carriage train to stop. Cruising into the station the carriages stopped right in front of us, with it all too obvious that there was not a single person aboard (apart from the driver!). We dithered as to what to do next. There was no point in getting on the train as we had no idea where Adrian and Derek were, so we apologised to the train driver and left him to go on his way.

Complete with suitcases, we made our way back to the car. Swinging into the car park, we could see little Pete's car – our handy man at the Centre who also does our cleaning in the mornings. Adrian had phoned from his mobile telephone explaining what had happened. Never trust a man (!) – they had got to the station earlier than Adrian had expected and managed to catch the 7.10 train to London, which we did not even know about, and which did not stop at Highbridge – and anyway, we weren't there by the time the train flashed through.

Adrian, realising a mistake had been made, panicked and bundled Derek off the train at the next station which was Weston-super-Mare. Leaving Derek happily sitting reading a paper, Adrian had raced round to the ticket office to see if there was a chance for us to get through to Weston in time to catch a connecting train which would still allow us to be in London in time for the Euro Tunnel. On getting the details, he telephoned through to the farm managing to catch Pete, who had duly driven out to the station to tell us. We had exactly 25 minutes to get to Weston-super-Mare for the connection.

Driving somewhat fast to Weston, we arrived in time to see Derek still happily reading the paper, completely oblivious of all the panicking that was going on around him. He was quite surprised to see us walking into the station with the suitcases, and although it had not gone quite to plan it all worked out very well.

At last settling back in the carriage, waving goodbye to Barry and a shattered Adrian, I was able to explain it all to Derek, show him the tickets, and then it was just a question of sit back and let the weekend happen.

The experience of Euro Tunnel was exciting, with champagne served with the meal as the train started to make its journey to Paris. It did not seem long at all before we were through the tunnel and into the French countryside. Certainly the countryside that we travelled through seemed very productive and gave the impression that the French were as guilty as ourselves in the removal of hedgerows. The farm buildings looked smaller and more scattered. With tremendous speed, it was not very long before we were entering the very smart and modern station in Paris.

We were transported to our hotel, and Friday evening was free for exploring the local surroundings with plenty of places to eat. We strolled around, eventually settling for a restaurant where guitar music was being played. With memories of schoolgirl

French lessons and plenty of sign language, we ordered our meal. The weather was very good and many of the locals were making the most of the tables and chairs dotted around the eating establishments. Just the chatter of a foreign language and the thoughts of a carefree weekend with no responsibilities were enough to lift our spirits.

The fact that the hotel was probably built on top of the Metro station, as it seemed to shake every time a train went through, we had already decided would not spoil our weekend. As pretty sound sleepers, we doubted that it would keep us awake, and indeed it didn't.

Saturday was a completely free day. Paris is very similar to London inasmuch as Paris has the Metro and London has the Underground. Everyone had been given a map of the Metro with all the stations marked for the typical sightseers' venues, and we had a wonderful day just roaming around seeing the Arc de Triomphe, walking up the Champs Elysées, seeing the Louvre – which was a quick glimpse because there are so many paintings in there that it would take more than a day to see them all – and of course, the Eiffel Tower.

I chickened out on the second floor but Derek went right to the top and said that the view was fantastic. The fact that it was another sunny day enhanced the beautiful gardens and endless fountains. One can appreciate why it is called a romantic city with so many lovely features. It is, of course, cosmopolitan, just as London is, but there are many customs and traditions that appear 'quaint' to the newcomer. Typical that one of my memories has to be the brass pictures of dogs on the pavement with arrows to the gutter, making dog-walkers aware that they should make the dogs foul in the gutter and not on the pavement. Two very tired but happy people returned to their hotel on the second night.

The next day, which was Sunday, we only had half a day as we needed to return to the hotel for the coach to take us to the concert. We again took the Metro and went to a place where they held a Sunday market. As we came out of the underground railway, the air was filled with birdsong. Row upon row of stalls were all in place with many, many varieties of canaries and finches. The French are very fond of caged birds and the designs of some of the cages were really beautiful, although it has to be said that some of them were not very big.

Different kinds of seed, feeders, fresh greenery and herbs were all sold to the caring bird owner. It was wonderful to see the colours of the canaries, ranging from the beautiful yellow, through to orange and some almost a brilliant red. Lovebirds, parakeets and even parrots competed to be heard above the general chatter of the buyers and sellers. Added to this were the many flower stalls, with many bouquets already gift-wrapped complete with curling ribbons, and the aroma of rose buds and carnations – a riot of colour, noise and smells such that one could fully understand the desire of an artist to try and capture such a scene on canvas.

With time to explore a nearby chapel with many stained glass windows, we enjoyed a coffee in a nearby square before revisiting the market for our return journey to the hotel.

Like good little holiday-makers, we were shepherded on to the coach ready for the concert. Because of the vast numbers attending we were dropped off at 4 p.m., despite the fact that the show gates did not open until 6 p.m., to give us a chance to get in the queue! The show was meant to start with Bruce Springsteen at 7.30 p.m., and by the time we had our seats it was nearly that time. But the people continued to come in and the show did not start.

Derek laughed at my concern that, as the seats were all taken, people started to sit on the stairs between the rows of seats and it became impossible to get out from anywhere. Still the show did not start, and by 8.45 p.m., having all got rather tired of the Mexican wave (!), clapping and stamping of feet was the order of the day to voice the disquiet at nothing happening.

It must be my age, but I could just see what was going to happen if a fight broke out and I was beginning to feel very uncomfortable. Derek thought this was all very funny but I think he was as relieved as me when the concert started, straight in with Tina Turner. No announcement as to where 'dear little Brucie' got to – but there you go! The show that Tina Turner put on and the stage effects were so good that the wait was completely forgotten about, and I'm sure that on the way out, if anyone had said 'I wonder what happened to Bruce Springsteen?', the response would have been 'who?'.

It was all well worth the wait, and even the fairly long journey home the next day could not distract from a very lovely and unforgettable weekend – in every way!

The year before we had been lucky enough to go to Greece. I have to be honest and say that I'm not a great lover of going abroad to hot countries to soak up sea and sun, whereas Derek loves the warm weather and misses the fact of really being able to enjoy our summers as we are always so busy.

Going to Greece was therefore left to Derek to organise – all I had to do, so I was told, was to pack my bags. It is always a mad rush to get away from our place, be it for a couple of days or a fortnight, so late the evening before our departure, I was still tying up loose ends of paperwork and writing out all the instructions for while we were away.

Luckily Simon was at home then, so he and Nikki, his girlfriend, were to look after the house and Centre in our absence. It was late October, so as far as wildlife was concerned, it would be fairly quiet.

Busy typing in my office, I was unaware that it was nearly midnight. Derek was in the bedroom packing, saying all the usual manly things such as 'Where's my . . .' and 'Have you seen . . .' and 'I can't find . . .' in his usual capable way. Then, with an attempt at being efficient, he collected the tickets and details together. It was then that I heard the worrying question of 'Do you know where our passports are?'

'But, I thought I'd said about checking them weeks ago', I said, panicking.

'I know,' replied Derek, 'I just forgot.'

Searching through the filing cabinet, I was pleased to see the passport in the right place but I had a horrible sneaking suspicion that it might be out of date – and I was right.

Having been in a similar situation a long time ago in my teens, I knew it was possible to go to the passport office and get one the same day but we were going to need photographs. Remembering the photo booth in Bridgwater, we got into the car and 1 a.m. found us in a deserted High Street in the middle of the town waiting for our pictures to develop.

'If we get all the information together as soon as we get home, we can leave tomorrow for Cardiff and see if it is possible to turn it round in time for our flight at 19.30 hrs', I said. Derek did not look convinced.

By early next morning, I had telephoned the passport office and been told that as long as we took all our details with us, we should be able to obtain our passports in time for our holiday.

Both Derek and I needed to go, so leaving Simon and Debbie to cope for an extra day, we dashed off to Cardiff. It was as well that this had all been Derek's fault as he found it hard to lose his temper with me when we arrived in Cardiff, only to find that I had left all the details on the kitchen table at home!

We did not have the time to physically drive home and back again and still hope to get the passports, so we decided to get Simon to drive over with the paperwork, thereby reducing the time to one journey only. Thank goodness for mobile phones, for within minutes a tutting Simon was on his way with the details.

When he arrived he had the broadest of smiles on his face having witnessed the stupidity of his parents. 'I don't know,' he chided as he walked towards us, handing over the paperwork, 'when will you both learn to be independent and think for yourselves instead of expecting me to sort out your problems.'

The rest of the day was a whirlwind of obtaining passports, finishing packing, panicking over the final instructions and an all-too-fast drive to the airport by son Simon, whose driving, at times, leaves a lot to be desired. White-faced from all the rushing (and maybe the driving too!), we at last arrived with minutes to spare to register for our flight. Waving a very appreciative good-bye to Simon as he drove away, we turned to enter the departure lounge – to join the rest of the passengers in a four-hour wait for our delayed flight!

It was a lovely holiday in a self-catering unit, giving us the freedom to sleep for as long as we wanted and eat when we wanted. Two weeks of sun, sea and many beautiful sights of Roman ruins, churches and a chance to see the Greeks' cultural way of life.

One of the abiding memories has to be a beautiful boat trip out to one of the many other small islands. With the water so clear, the fish could be seen in the depths below and we were lucky enough to sight dolphins as they leaped in the water and circled the boat. What is it about these mammals that takes one's breath away with the sheer excitement of seeing them? Their closeness caused many on the boat to be almost in tears with emotion. Sadly, they were not to stay with us for long and we were unable to follow them as they moved into Turkish waters where our boat was not allowed to go.

How sad that we have drawn lines across the world, ones that are unseen by wildlife – yet to be on one side or the other can mean safety or death depending on the 'owner's' beliefs as to whether nature is to be valued, exploited or destroyed.

The boat went on to moor by a small island for a barbecue lunch and everyone swam in the transparent blue sea where the marine life could be seen so easily. A lazy return trip, with local songs played by a couple of boatmen with guitars, made it one of the days that was hard to beat.

The island that we were staying on was very flat and many of the visitors hired bikes to get around. One day, we decided to do the same. The owner endeavoured to explain the cost of the hire: apparently, it was only £3 per day for a bike with no gears, and £5 a day for a bike with gears. Derek, ever the one to save money, considered that if the island was flat, then there was no need for gears. The man tried to help the discussion by flapping his leg along the side of the bike, but we failed to understand his meaning.

'I think we can manage without the gears', said Derek.

The man dragged his foot along the ground once more. I was beginning to understand what he meant.

A scooter complete with dog on the driver's lap, and what appeared to be his granny sitting side-saddle on the back.

103

'I would prefer the ones with gears', I mused.

'Why,' said Derek, 'when the island is so flat?'

'I have a funny feeling, that as well as having no gears on the cheaper bikes,' I said slowly, trying to read the expression on the owner's face, who was studying me to see if I understood his wild gestures, 'they do not have brakes either!'

The bike shop owner nodded his head excitedly – I understood. Thumbs up and big smile. We took the £5 bikes!

Derek rode in front with me pedalling behind. At the first roundabout, he had to brake hard as a scooter complete with dog on the driver's lap, and what appeared to be his granny sitting side-saddle on the back, shot across in front of him.

'What a good job we've got brakes' was the smart comment from behind.

We rode towards the local wildlife reserve to which the travel representative had given us directions. He stated that the only thing he had seen, when he went along there, was a dead dog so we were full of anticipation. Well, we certainly saw more than he had. (This is what happens when one has such a trained eye!) We saw the dead dog, still there although probably in an even sorrier state than when he had seen it, plus a dead cat and a dead goat, which did somewhat detract from the many beautiful views. Sun, sea and sand – but give me Britain anytime!

Another outing to a local fishing village was really interesting, and the seafront was alive with the fishermen mending their nets and unloading their catches. Further along several restaurants barbecued fresh sardines, a local speciality. We sauntered along the front, where the smell of the smoked food enticed us into one of the eating places along the harbour front. I don't have a liking for fish so chose an omelette, but Derek ordered the traditional five sardines, cooked in a way that he relished. It had been a long time since he had enjoyed a fish dish so much. Relaxing after our meal, we took in the local banter and the colourful displays of the souvenir stalls dotted around the quayside.

The smoke from the barbecues added to the haze of the midday sun and we were thankful of the brightly coloured bunting that offered shelter to the diners. Suitably refreshed, we decided to walk further along the harbour front to the main town.

Several boats were going up and down and the larger ferries could be seen further out, taking tourists back to the mainland.

The water was so clear that it was easy to see shoals of fish as they swam around the harbour edge, and we mused that catching them for the tourists could not be too difficult a task. Further along, as we neared the town, the water became almost black with the fish that were twisting and diving in a feeding frenzy. It was hard to see why so many fish should be attracted to this area and we walked up and down trying to see what was causing this behaviour. Then slowly, it dawned on us. We were standing by the area where the effluent from the town was discharged into the sea, which was obviously being recycled by the marine life. I, for one, was very glad that I had not had sardines for my lunch!

My happiest holidays are spent at Lyme Regis. Whenever we go there, it's always like going home. There is a flat overlooking the Cobb which we often hire, mainly in the winter, and in a way, we enjoy doing all the ordinary things that we rarely get the chance to do – to drift along the promenade towards the shops, browse round the bookstalls, walk along the cliffs or just walk by the sea.

Even on cold, wet and windy days, the sea is magnificent as it crashes against the sea defences. The following day there will be shells to discover, beautiful driftwood and different coloured seaweeds dredged from the bottom of the sea by the turbulent waves. And after a walk sorting through these 'riches', what better than a cream tea in one of the local tearooms set in this picturesque town, so often used for film sets. There is time to sit and watch television, read books, cook proper meals and time for Derek and myself just to have each other to ourselves for a while. But then, after a week or so, even though I can feed the seagulls with bread and watch the ducks in the river mouth, I'm ready to go home – I miss my animals.

Even in just those few days in Paris, the cubs seem to have grown and it was soon going to be time to move them out of the kitchen. Ebony and Barley, being the youngest, were still on three feeds a day but the rest were mainly on what I call support bottles – just topping them up as they changed to solid food. Meadow, being a slow feeder, was one of the cubs that I was really pleased to see starting to take solid foods.

Taffy, David and Eric were practically completely weaned. Mealtimes were an event, with plenty of barging with their shoulders to keep other cubs at bay while they ate the tasty morsel that they had pinched from the food bowls.

Back into the routine the next day of bottle-feeding the younger cubs while the older ones fight over their food, Debbie popped her head around the door and laughed at my somewhat disarrayed appearance.

'Glad to be home?' she remarked, laughing. 'By the way, Bill's been on the phone. He wants to know when "Kidner woman" is going to take him out!'

I smiled, 'I'll give him a ring – perhaps he would like to come out and see the badger cubs.'

'Oooh, I doubt it', laughed Debbie. 'The only good badger . . .'

'. . . is a dead badger', I joined in and with that, she was gone.

Bill Groves is a farmer who lives in the village of Othery. Despite being over 70 and not really looking after himself very well, he looks very fit and healthy. He hates badgers and for good reason, as each year he suffers a lot of corn damage to his fields where they eat it or roll and flatten the corn as they play. Unfortunately, his neighbour has allowed the setts in his field to increase dramatically, so much so that in two of the fields, almost a quarter of the land is taken up by badger setts.

Even if the landowner was prepared to obtain a licence to move these setts back into the hedgerow, which it is possible to do within the legislation of the Badger Act, it would now cost a great deal of money to carry out the work to rectify his problem and the farmer is not prepared to pay for this. In a way, with the law as it is, it is a no-win situation which will never go away.

Many farmers are unaware that is possible to shut down setts under licence as soon as they appear in the field, before it becomes a big problem. Indeed, many badger groups are prepared to help obtain licences and will guide farmers to make sure that the closure of setts is done properly. Hopefully this will achieve a result that is acceptable to both the farmer and the badger.

I have in the past shut a couple of sett entrances down for Bill under licence with the help of Adrian Coward, who is far more knowledgeable in these matters than me. But through our contact, Bill and I have fallen into a loose arrangement of having lunch together every other month so that Bill can complain about his badgers and I can sympathise.

With the cubs fed and sound asleep, I telephoned Bill.

'Hello', answered the gruff voice after a few rings.

'Hello, Bill, it's Pauline, how are you?' I asked.

'Ah, Kidner woman, what's all this traipsing off to Paris no less, leaving me behind all on my own?' he complained.

'I had a very nice time thank you, and had no worries about you being on your own, knowing full well about the entourage of woman friends that you have scattered across Somerset', I teased.

'I have a few, I have a few', he boasted.

'Didn't you ever get married, Bill?' I enquired.

'Well,' he drawled, 'you know I lived with my mother, well, when I was in my late twenties, she said to me, "Bill, tis time you took yourself a wife", well,' he growled, 'I tried a couple in the village – but they both went back to their husbands, so I didn't bother after that!'

'Bill, you are awful', I stated, and he chuckled.

'When are we going out for lunch? I'm feeling very neglected', he asked.

'Well,' I countered, 'it's not so long before the Bath and West Show and, no doubt, you will be going to cause trouble at the NFU tent and the Badger Group stand this year, won't you?'

'Indeed I will, and for the reporter at the *Western Daily Press*', Bill added. 'Did you hear the other day, the Queen requested that she didn't want any reporters when she went away on holiday? Well, I wrote to her and said that I didn't want badgers on my land but I have to put up with it, and what was she going to do about that. Didn't even bother to reply – got some secretary or other to write back. If she didn't want any reporters, why should I have badgers on my land? There's only one good badger and that's a dead badger!'

I could tell the conversation was going downhill.

'Well, Bill, I'll see you on the Thursday by the Badger Group stand at 12.30 and we'll have lunch together. How's that?' I asked.

'Ought to be allowed to shoot the damn things, never had any problems when we used to shoot about 20 each year. Too many of the things, there's only one . . .'

'How's the cat?' I said, quickly changing the subject.

'She's fine', said Bill.

'Good,' I countered, 'see you at the Bath and West then?'

'It's a few weeks until then', he complained.

'Unless you want to come over here and spend some time with my cubs?' I innocently asked.

'No,' came the gruff reply, 'see you then.' The phoned banged down, but I knew he would be there on the Thursday as promised.

Sue McMillan, from the BBC Natural History Unit in Bristol, contacted me to see if we would be prepared to be part of a series called 'Nature Detectives'. They wished to show the rehabilitation of badger cubs, our protocol and their final release. I was surprised as I knew that this was already being followed by Mike Gunton for the series 'Back to the Wild', but this was not a problem.

The kitchen, yet again, was therefore invaded with film cameras and crew. It is easy to see why the filmmakers love to do badgers as the very crew themselves became enchanted with them and the patience to obtain the right footage is immediately there; and I have no problem with filming as long as the animals' interest is the first concern.

Fitting in with the feeding regime that the cubs were used to, the crew were able to capture the fun and games of the big boys, Meadow, Eric and David, as they played with empty cereal packets and tugged at an old shoe as well as the kitchen rug. Ebony and Barley, not quite so strong on their legs, tried their best to join in and excelled themselves when given a roll of kitchen paper which they duly destroyed.

They were able to film the bottle-feeding of the smaller guys whilst seeing the free-for-all for the solid food with the older cubs. And finally, tired from playing and with tummies full, it was easy to capture the cubs sound asleep behind the chair and the kitchen was quiet again for a few hours. The next visit from this film crew would be to see the tattooing and testing prior to going into the grassed enclosures at West Hatch, and then their final release.

Just as Glade was the main character in the first group, Taffy was to be the 'star' in the resident kitchen crew. Ironic that both should have been discarded by humans involved with digging for badgers, and that both should now be used in a televised attempt to entertain and educate humans. One can only hope that knowledge and understanding will eventually reduce the persecution that exists today.

Sarah's tiny fox cub, Woody, had survived with all her loving care, and indeed was now joined by three other weaned fox cubs that had come in over the last couple of weeks. It was now no longer necessary for Woody to go home with Sarah at the end of the day and he too was starting to eat solid food, so it was time for them all to leave the pen in the hospital room and go to larger facilities at the RSPCA's unit at West Hatch.

The change of environment would give the cubs far more space and certainly, as far as Woody was concerned, the break from Sarah, as his carer, would help him eventually become wild again so that he could be released. Most of the volunteers working in the hospital room were happy to see the fox cubs go – not because they didn't like them but because the smell from four fox cubs is very pungent, to say the least!

This is one of the main reasons why people, who mistakenly think fox cubs will make good pets, quickly change their minds. But sometimes the damage is done and the fox cubs can already be too tame ever to be released; then the cubs have to spend the rest of their lives in captivity or be put to sleep. It is essential, therefore, that fox cubs are reared sensibly with a view to returning them to the wild.

No longer the dark chocolate brown of young fox cubs, the youngsters now had their red coats. Pointed ears and noses expressed interest as we opened their pen. They really looked like tiny foxes now. I helped Sarah catch the cubs and put them into cages ready for their journey down to the RSPCA centre. The cubs trilled with their yelping bark to show that they were confused by our actions. We covered the cages with blankets to make the cubs feel more secure while they travelled. Quickly putting them into the car, we were soon on our way towards Taunton. It was not the nicest of days, with rain drizzling, making the motorway part of the journey difficult with the spray from the lorries and cars making it hard to see. The windscreen wipers monotonously ticked away.

Sarah had wanted to see them go to their new home and I made light conversation as I could see that, emotionally, she was going to find it hard to say goodbye to 'her' fox cub that she had spent so much time with. You cannot spend the hours that are required to help a small helpless baby grow into an independent youngster without becoming attached, and it is even harder when the aim is to return the animal back to the wild. No one can guarantee that they will survive, that they will stay healthy and find somewhere to live permanently, and it is so easy to choose the easy option of denying them freedom for your own peace of mind. Time and time again, when working with wildlife, you need to question whether you are doing it for the animal or doing it for yourself because each will bring a different answer.

All too quickly, we arrive and are greeted by Colin Seddon, the manager at the Wildlife Centre. Colin has been at West Hatch for many years and we are lucky to have someone with such experience to help us with our orphans. We can bring them to his centre knowing that they will be given the best chance of survival, as Colin goes to great pains to ensure that release sites are suitable, where an animal can sustain itself and have the best chance to survive.

At the moment the cubs were to go into a pen with other fox cubs, but within a couple of days, they would be going into the large grassed enclosure to learn how to forage and survive prior to being released. Carrying the cages into the unit, Colin chatted to Sarah and me, saying how there seemed to be a lot of badger cubs this year and it would be some time before he could take the next group of cubs from me. I suggested that maybe the kitchen crew that were still with us could go into the observation sett and enclosure which was now empty, having lost Bluebell. At least it would give them more space until such time as Colin could take them.

Walking past the array of pens and aviaries, I was envious of the facilities. I so wished that we were able to have more pens. It would make everything so much easier and better for the animals that came to our care. Sadly, money always seems very slow in coming in for the care of wildlife.

We stopped by a pen with a long outside run deep in shavings where fox cubs quickly scuttled under cover as we approached. There was also an indoor area that the cubs could use if it was cold.

'This is much better than what they've been used to, isn't it?' I asked Sarah, trying to make it a bit easier for her.

She nodded, she knew what I meant.

'Time to say goodbye', I said, as we put the cages down. 'Sarah has done a really good job with the cubs – they look really chunky and well.'

'They look fine', agreed Colin as we took them out of the cages and put them in with the others.

With the briefest of kisses, Sarah caressed Woody's body to her face. Eyes shining as the tears welled, Sarah placed him on the floor. The cubs scattered; one that had been hiding under an overturned dog basket came out and yapped in excitement at the newcomers and then skidded quickly back inside on seeing the three watching humans. Another came out and trilled a greeting as our group took advantage of the huge space and ran to find the perimeters of their new pen.

Having watched to see that all was well, we made our way back to the car.

'How's Glade and Co. getting on?' I asked.

'Glade's still a bit tame', said Colin. 'It's always a problem when they come in very small and have to be hand-reared and, of course, with the television crew following them for the series, he has become everyone's favourite. But we are stopping anyone from going down to the paddocks and changing our routines. That usually does the trick.'

'He was always very bold as a cub,' I said, 'that's why I wanted to move him on to you so quickly. I hope he'll be OK.'

It was my turn to look worried. Two very quiet people drove home, each with their own thoughts and concerns.

Griff and Gruff

It always seems that as soon as one animal goes, another arrives, and when we eventually got home Ellie, who was on Reception, excitedly told us about the two ugly kittens that someone had brought in. Ellie is one of our animal care assistants. Still a teenager, she is bright and bubbly with her long brown hair usually tied up in a ponytail. Ellie is one of the few members of staff that likes the terrapins and loves snakes too, so for Ellie to say the kittens were ugly – they really must be!

Sarah and I made our way up to the staff room, and there were two of the ugliest black kittens that I have ever seen. They looked more like gremlins. Dumped in a cardboard box, they had been brought in by a passerby – not that we take in domestic animals, but the fact that we now have ten cats does perhaps tell the tale that we are rather soft when given a sob story! Griff and Gruff were to become permanent residents of the staff room, together with all the other cats, taking advantage of mealtimes when most of the staff have packed lunches that they will share.

The next day started well with the arrival of long-awaited correspondence from Simon and Nikki. Their year in Australia was going well, having started in Sydney, then moving on to Melbourne which just had to include a visit to 'Ramsay Street'! After their first two months staying with friends and relations, they had started to tour having bought a van to travel and live in. We certainly did not envy them for the back-breaking jobs that they had to take to find enough money to survive, but some of the wonderful places that they went to must have been fantastic.

Both Nikki and Simon wrote (although one has to say that Nikki was more consistent) and it was great fun to hear about their exploits. Nikki's first letter to my parents was duly returned to Australia with comments from my father that the letter had contained two spelling mistakes and a double negative – he had always teased Nikki for her spelling mistakes when she had worked in our Reception! They were obviously enjoying life and getting on well together.

Dear parents,
Greetings! We have left the Perth District and are travel-
ling northbound. We stopped at Monkey Mia to meet
some dolphins and are soon to hit Coral Bay – good
snorkelling area. The weather is warming up and the van
is running smoothly. The mozzies have resurfaced which is
a bit vexing – Nikki's covered in bumps! – but we're
surviving . . .
. . . Since my birthday, I have spent many a happy hour
drilling holes and making pallets for what could be loosely
described as a wage . . .
We popped into Torongo Zoo which is set on a nearby
mountain. Nikki was fortunate enough to stroke a baby
Koala bear which kept her quiet for a couple of hours. We
also got a glimpse of the wonderful poisonous reptiles that
frequent this fly ridden country . . .
Nikki is not getting many hours a week at S & N Ltd so
is not earning very much at the moment, but is leaps and
bounds ahead in the spending department – she still
doesn't understand that although a dress for 30 dollars was
a superb bargain, it was still no way as cheap as nothing. It
is still very dangerous to walk the streets during shopping
hours especially with the seasonal 'SALES' . . .

. . . I must now regrettably stop writing as I have run out of things to tell you and I've been up since 4.30 a.m. and am ready for bed. Feel free to pass this letter on to whoever I haven't written to for a while and also to Grandad to correct and grade!

Love to you all,
Simon and Nikki

Having sat down with a cup of coffee to read the letter, I was running behind time. I was off to a school in Surrey to give a talk and I still had all the equipment – projector, slides and screen – to get into the car. John was on Reception and is well used to dealing with a variety of calls, from enquiries about opening times and prices, to reporting injured animals and even calls for advice. Just as I was dashing through Reception to get away, a rather embarrassed John stopped me.

'I've just had a phone call about a tortoise, and I know you're in a hurry but I think it's quite important', he said hesitantly.

'Oh, John,' I wailed, 'if I don't go soon, I'm going to be late . . .'

'I know, it's just that . . .' His face coloured and he wasn't sure how to explain his problem.

'Quickly then, John,' I said, 'I really must go!'

'Well,' he said laughing nervously, and dropping his voice he whispered, 'I've had this lady on the phone who's got a male tortoise and . . .' – he looked around to see if anyone was in earshot – 'it's had its penis out for over 24 hours and the lady thinks it has got stuck out and she doesn't know what to do.'

Suppressing my mirth, I matter-of-factly stated, 'Oh, that's easy, telephone her back and tell her to make sure that it is clean and then lubricate the penis with oil or Vaseline and it will soon pop back. And if that doesn't do the trick, she ought to ring the vet.'

'I can't do that . . .' faltered John.

'Course you can', I said, and with that sailed off to the car park. I must admit it kept me smiling for the rest of the day.

The next day, when I knew John was on duty in Reception, I rang through on the internal line. 'Reception', John answered.

'Oh,' I breathed down the phone, 'is that the penis expert?!'

'You!' spluttered John. 'The things I do for you – I don't know why I stay here!'

'Because you enjoy it', I retorted, laughed and put the phone down.

My sense of humour has also at times got me into trouble and there was another occasion with John where I left him embarrassed. I was in Reception looking through the post and John answered the phone. I could tell from his serious voice that it was quite important. John sympathised and nodded, listening with great care to the caller's problem.

Eventually John asked the caller to wait while he found out some information for him, and placing his hand over the mouthpiece of the telephone, John turned to me to explain the situation. Looking very serious, he said: 'It's a man who has found a dead pigeon in his garden but he doesn't know what to do as it's got rings on its toes.'

Sadly, I have a very over-active imagination and sometimes a very sick sense of humour. My mind conjured up this picture of a pigeon lying on its back with its feet in the air, diamond rings flashing on each toe and a watch further up its leg – and the more I tried to get this ridiculous image out of my mind and explain to John what to do, the more I started to laugh until eventually I was crying. The look of complete surprise on John's face as to why a dead pigeon should be so amusing did nothing to help me control myself, and I just had to leave and stand outside while a very confused John explained to the caller that he would ring him back with information a little later.

I hasten to add that when I had come to my senses, I did indeed ring the caller back with sensible advice and proper sympathy.

. . . a dead pigeon with rings on its toes

By the end of May the kitchen crew were in need of space, and now that they were fully weaned, it was time to move them into our observation sett on the farm. Originally built for Bluebell, Willow and Primrose, there was plenty of room with the three indoor chambers and an outside enclosure 40 feet square. Here the cubs would have space to dig at night and could even bathe in the pond.

We moved them all down first thing in the morning, placing them in the chambers that had been filled with fresh straw. The first hour was spent exploring, with Ebony and Barley, the smallest cubs, scampering around well after Meadow, Eric, Taffy and David had decided to go to sleep. Popping their heads first into one chamber and then the next, it almost appeared that they were putting on a show for Derek, myself and Sarah as we watched through the glass. Surprisingly, none of them ventured out into the daylight and soon even the last two tired, choosing to sleep in the same chamber as everyone else. Ebony and Barley hauled themselves on top of the other four and promptly, after a yawn and a stretch, fell asleep too.

The kitchen felt very empty as I returned upstairs but I had to admit that it would be nice to give the room just one more clean and know that it would stay cleaner a little bit longer without my black and white friends. The locks could come off the cupboards, no more barricading the fridge at night and I was really looking forward to seeing them out in the enclosure that evening.

Now nearly into June, the evenings were getting longer and it was well past 9 p.m. before the cubs started to stir. Inquisitive faces peeped from the tunnels but eventually it was the sound of my voice that gave them the confidence to come out and explore the compound. Then the fun really started as they ran and cavorted around in the grass, clambering on to the large tree trunks and then disappearing back down the tunnels. Meadow was running so fast that he took a turning into the pond, and the shock of entering the water made him stick his hair up so that he looked like a wet snowball. The other cubs ran up towards this dripping spectacle and then charged off in the opposite direction.

I was the first to tire and made my way back to the house, leaving them to enjoy the night in the moonlight in their new temporary home.

7

Never Again

The cubs were very happy in their new home and made the most of the enclosure to dig and play. I went down with them most evenings, just to put the food in and to make sure that they were all getting their fair share of it.

Taffy, being the oldest of the group, took the lead. The activities of preening and musking were part of their initial behaviour as soon as they came out from the observation sett. The musking of my shoes showed that I was well and truly part of their group, but it was good to see that if other people were around, the cubs were not so keen to come into the enclosure. When the camera crew came to film some of their behaviour now they were in an outside pen, they had to film from outside the walls to gain any footage.

Squeak

Caroline Gould from the Vale Rescue Centre in Gloucestershire rang me to ask if we could take some of their cubs for release.

This seemed to be a year when there were a lot of cubs around. She also had a badger called Squeak from the previous year which was too tame to be released and, despite being very attached to her, Caroline did not have any facilities large enough to give her the chance to exercise and play. She wondered, seeing as I had lost Bluebell, whether we would be prepared to give her a permanent home.

I was unsure if this was the right thing to do, as sometimes just moving a badger from one carer to another can change them back to being wild. But I offered to put Squeak in with Taffy's crew and see how she got on. If she remained too tame, then she could stay with us when the other cubs moved on.

Caroline came a couple of weeks later together with her partner Martin. Beside bringing Squeak and the two young cubs for release, it was a chance for them both to have a couple of hours off. The Vale Rescue Centre is a much bigger place than ours, dealing just with wildlife casualties. We are lucky that, with the RSPCA at West Hatch, we have a nearby facility that can help us but with the Vale, they take from quite a large area and it keeps them very, very busy.

The two young cubs were placed in one of the casualty pens. There were three other pens already holding groups of four or five badger cubs in each. Caroline and Martin then carried Squeak down to the observation sett to meet Taffy and Co. Taking Squeak out of the box, Caroline sat with her on her lap. She was indeed a very tame and pretty badger and I could see that Caroline was feeling very emotional at leaving her with us.

It is always such a responsibility when someone passes on to you an animal that means so much to them, and I always worry in case things go wrong. I felt honoured that Caroline held me in high enough esteem to feel she could leave her with me, and it was lovely to have a badger that I could handle and stroke in the same way that Bluebell allowed. Pushing Squeak gently through the door in by the chambers, she sniffed at the strong smell of badgers; the cubs immediately woke up and sat with ears pricked, having heard the bolt on the door being pushed across.

All the three chambers are interconnected and dressed with real tree root and earth-coloured cement, so it gives the impression of being underground. I had put the large light on so that we could see the areas surrounding the chambers where the cubs could still move about under cover, so that we could see what was going to happen. We watched from the viewing windows where the public usually stand, where they are able to see what goes on in the chambers.

Taffy and Meadow were the first to tumble out of the chamber to meet the older badger. We hoped that, as a young female, she would take to the cubs. She greeted them vocally as they came towards her and each in turn backed on to her and musked her flanks as a sign of acceptance.

David and Eric joined in the welcome party, but Ebony hesitated slightly, not sure of this large badger that had suddenly entered their home. She went back into the chamber and waited, listening to all the sound of movement outside. Taffy and Meadow returned to the chamber – after all, it was only another badger! They settled down to sleep but Ebony remained unsure.

David and Eric followed Squeak, who checked every corner and eventually found the chamber where the other cubs were – Meadow and Taffy now sound asleep. Dropping into the chamber, Squeak met with Ebony and started to preen through her fur. Encouraged by this greeting, Ebony returned the gesture as David and Eric flopped into the chamber to tussle with each other in the restricted space. Eventually lying down by Meadow and Taffy, Squeak settled with the other cubs on top of her.

'Well,' I said to Caroline and Martin, 'that was easy, they all seem to be OK. But I will monitor them tonight to check if things are still alright.'

We left the cubs to it and I had the chance to show Caroline and Martin around before it was time for them to make their way home. I know they had a last look before leaving to make sure Squeak was alright. It must have been very hard for them to say goodbye.

It was the beginning of June, baby bird season, and the time when endless youngsters are brought in as casualties. It is hard to get across to the general public that often it is better to leave fledged birds alone as usually the parents are nearby still feeding them, and it is only because the birds have moved out from the nest on to the branches that their calls are misconstrued as calls for being lost – whereas all they are trying to do is to make sure they get fed first!

Mike Hollist

HEDGEHOG TEENAGER

Ken Chapman

BEAUTY THE ROE FAWN

PAULINE AND GLADE - A SPECIAL RELATIONSHIP

GRIFF

"THE UGLY KITTENS"

GRUFF

Jason Venus

LONG-EARED BAT

Gary Sealey

HIMMY AND BERTHA, NOCTULE BATS

MURRAY, GENTLE GIANT WITH DAVID

)LD FRIENDS - GLADE WITH MURRAY

"KEEPING FIT!"

WEIGHING EVERY DAY SHOWS PROGRESS

Colin Seddon

HOW MUCH DO I WEIGH NOW?

PLAYTIME IN THE CUBBY-HOLE

MEADOW - HIDING IN THE CAMERA BAG

GLADE AT THREE WEEKS, TAFFY AT TEN DAYS

SLEEPING THE DAY AWAY

Already feathered, these young birds, if picked up, will usually die from shock and it really is best to leave them alone. However, dislodged nests and imminent danger from cats, dogs or cars mean there are still plenty of birds needing help. Birds are usually the one kind of animal very often incorrectly identified. I can remember Simon quite excitedly going off for a baby heron a year or so ago. We had never reared a baby heron, so were looking forward to having the chance of trying. Simon had quite a long way to go to fetch it, so it was a good two hours before he returned.

I happened to be in Reception as the car drew up and it was obvious by the look on his face as he came in that – it was not a baby heron.

'It's a baby pigeon, I have driven over 50 miles for a baby pigeon!' he sighed.

'Well,' I tried to reason, 'if it needs help it doesn't matter what it is . . .'

'How can anyone think that a baby pigeon was a baby heron?' He was not to be pacified.

'You have to admit that baby pigeons do look rather different before all their feathers come through, and one could think that the beak was longer than for a pigeon', I reasoned.

'But the legs,' he countered, 'didn't they think that the legs would be just a little bit longer? You know what's going to happen, don't you?' He looked accusingly at me. 'This will be another success, which will join the other 250 that we have sitting on the roof right at this moment!'

He marched off – sometimes he did sound just like Derek.

But he was right. We have got rather too many pigeons around and I hadn't realised that they were having problems finding places to nest until I went into our bedroom the other day. That's funny, I thought to myself, picking up a couple of feathers lying on the counterpane of the bed. Moving over to the open window, I let the feathers fall. I was doing housework, and I hadn't long finished in that room; they must have blown in from the window.

Going out of the bedroom, I started to sort out the piles of ironing and carried Derek's shirts back into the bedroom to put in the wardrobe. We have quite a lot of big, heavy antique furniture and our wardrobe is the kind with two mirrored doors with drawers in between, sitting on a plinth with an ornate top to it. I opened one of the mirrored doors and as I went to put a shirt

. . . a pigeon nursery in his bedroom . . .

on to a hanger, I felt something go over my head. Looking up, I noticed a beady eye looking down at me. With the following cooing sound, it did not take me long to realise that the 'something' was a pigeon that had flown in.

Standing back to survey the scene, I was amused to see one pigeon busy arranging feathers around her nest with her mate, who had just flown in complete with twig to assist with the building work. I saw little chance of Derek allowing a pigeon nursery in his bedroom and quickly evicted the two squatters, thankful that the nest was only in the early stages of creation – although I still felt guilty at disturbing them.

Luckily Derek never noticed that the bedroom window stayed closed for a few days to deter the ardent lovers or that, for a few weeks, my eyes tended to sweep the top of the furniture every time I walked into a room where the window had been left open!

Squeak continued to be accepted by the cubs – indeed, she was almost revered as a surrogate mum and I felt happier to step back and leave the badgers to themselves. I still checked them when I went down to put the feed in and was very concerned, one evening, to notice that the chain link fence at the front of the enclosure looked to be chewed. Looking closely, I could see that the fencing was being chewed from the outside. Along the front edge on the outside of the pen there is a small wall only about 2 feet high, and it was obvious that something was standing on the wall and having a go at the wire.

I was very concerned as I knew that we had a resident badger family living on the farm, some of which had been released from the enclosure in previous years, and it was possible that a male badger may be trying to get at the cubs, being upset at their presence within his territory, as they did not belong to his social group.

Luckily we have an external light that shines on the front of the enclosure so I arranged for the light to be left on at night, thereby making it possible to see what was going on from a bedroom at the top of our house. It worried me, but the chain link was very strong and I doubted that a badger could get through. We did occasionally see a badger on our farm, but not on a regular basis after Bluebell had died.

Even more badgers were being brought in and we were lucky that Linda Grove, the chairman of our charity, was also prepared to care for a group of badger cubs as our facilities were becoming very stretched. Linda has worked with us for many years, having first come to Secret World as a visitor, and is now very much an anchor person for all that goes on here. She is one of the many valued volunteers that we have, one who no matter what time of night or day, if asked to do a 'favour' – be it to collect a casualty, dress up in a badger suit or shake a collection box – if she can physically manage it, Linda will be there.

She has a stable near her house, where she is able to care for a small group of cubs. She is now very expert in cleaning up mess and scruffing cubs without being bitten, and is experienced in night-time feeds. Linda is also very supportive when things go wrong and she shared my sadness, as indeed did all of our staff and many, many visitors, when we found out that Gordon, our fox who had been with us for over thirteen years, was terminally ill.

Gordon came to us as a tame cub when we first started our Centre and had been a surrogate 'Dad' to many cubs and an old friend to our remaining foxes, Misty, Tag and Kevin. He would recognise my footsteps and, as I walked down to the badger sett, he would always be waiting for a fuss. Gordon had aged a lot in his last year, suffering from arthritis, so that we had to build a set of stairs for him to reach his favourite lay-up place over the door, and it was no real surprise when the vet told us that the time had come for us to put him to sleep. Well known for his love of Smarties, he is missed by us all and was quietly buried under the weeping willow tree in the courtyard.

I was very sad that we had been trying for so many years to get our foxes out into a grassed pen and it had taken us years to raise enough money to complete this project. It was ironic that he died in the same year that we reached our target – the fencing is now up and the foxes due to be moved. But then, especially in his final years, it may have been that a new environment would have been too much of a shock for him. Who can tell? But it was something that I regretted, that I was unable to achieve this in his lifetime.

Being the month of June also meant that the Bath and West Agricultural Show at Shepton Mallet was taking place. It is a very large show with judging of farm stock, agricultural machinery, flower tent, funfair rides and all the usual trade stands to be expected at such a large event.

The Somerset Trust Badger Group always has a stand there for the four days and usually Secret World has a stand there too, so one way or another I was going to be there manning a stall at some time or other, but on the Thursday – I had a date with Bill.

It was just the right weather for the show, glorious sunshine encouraging the sales of ice creams and lemonade, warm enough to tempt people to laze by the main ring and watch the horse jumping or the Evel Knievel jump bikes. Music pounded out from the village green, and screams of delight came from the brave who had risked the big wheel or the speed of the twisting joy-rides.

The sound of metal clanging as the farriers shoed horses or made intricate wrought iron ornaments almost drowned the commentary of the compere trying to whip up excitement as the sheep-shearing competition took place. All the men looked very hot as they struggled to hold the sheep in the heat and trim them at break-neck speed. It's a mixture of town and country people, there to enjoy themselves.

For the farmers, it's a chance to meet other farmers that they probably don't get the chance to see from one year to the next, either to show their animals or to admire other people's. A time to talk business, moan about prices – a general banter.

For the townfolk, it's a taste of the country, a chance to get close to farm animals, understand more about it and to see many of the wonderful crafts that skilled people are able to produce in small businesses. It's also time to have fun, find a bargain and taste all manner of foods that this country is able to produce. And the sun puts everybody in the right mood (apart from those selling umbrellas and raincoats!).

I made my way up the grassed aisle to the conservation area where the badger stand would be, and a voice in the distance told me I was nearly there.

'. . . should be able to do something about it. Too many of the damn things. You should buy some land and take all the badgers and keep them yourself if you like them so much. There's only one good badger and that's a dead badger!'

Bill was obviously already at the stand. Luckily, Adrian Coward was at the stand and he was used to Bill. It is not easy to man a stand at the show – there are some farmers who will come and complain, sometimes very vociferously, and it can be very upsetting when all you are trying to do is to reason and put the other side to an argument whilst still understanding that badgers do indeed cause problems.

Quite ironic in a way that farmers complain about too many badgers when it is not just legislation protecting them that has caused an increase. The growth of maize as a crop, drainage of land, several cuts of silage a year which keeps grass short for a much longer time, enabling badgers to forage for earthworms more easily, all play a part. And I've yet to believe the percentage increase as given in the last survey. Increased, yes, we see more of them – but please tell how you count all the holes and miraculously know how many badgers there are living underground?

As I arrived Bill was perched on the large Somerset Trust Badger Group sign.

'Look at this', said Adrian to me, stretching his arms out to show Bill sitting on the sign. 'I have had to take a photograph – Bill Groves supported by the Somerset Trust Badger Group!'

'Hmmph', Bill snorted. Despite the hot weather, Bill had on a sports jacket, white shirt and trousers with bracers. His strong wiry grey hair was combed in place and he scratched his full white beard, thinking of what to say next.

'Brilliant!' I laughed, and before Bill could enter into another torrent of anti-badger conversation, I quickly said, 'Come on, lunch!'

Linking his arm in mine, I guided Bill away, waving to Adrian over my shoulder.

'Where have you been so far?' I asked as we strolled towards the food tent.

'Well, I've been in the NFU tent and told them what a lot of nonsense they're talking, and I've been to the *Western Daily Press* office and seen that, what's her name, that Tina girl. I've told her that she should print my article – all this fuss about badgers and TB, what about all the corn damage, all the money I lose, who's going to pay for that, tell me!' Bill snapped at me, his blue eyes staring hard into my face.

'I wish I had an answer, Bill,' I said, 'but you know I don't. – Here, let's go in here.' And I steered him into the food tent to choose lunch.

'Is it your turn to pay or mine?' he asked gruffly.

'Well, at these prices, hopefully yours, but I think really it's my turn', I joked with him.

Bill will usually polish off ham, egg and chips . . . and bread and butter . . . and usually some of my chips as well. But today, he informed me, he was having to diet and therefore had ham salad. However, if Bill was on a diet, it was one I wouldn't have minded following as he proceeded to wade his way through a huge knickerbocker glory before finishing with coffee and cream!

Conversation was difficult with so much background noise as Bill has a job to hear – although I do think that sometimes his hearing is selective! But we chatted generally about his nephew, the spraying that needed to be done on his corn, and general chit-chat.

It was obvious from his sarcastic comments to people passing by that Bill knew many of the visitors to the show, and, I have to say, quite a few were young ladies. The old rascal certainly has his fair share of friends!

'Where are you going after lunch?' I asked.

'I want to see some of the machinery', said Bill.

I screwed my nose up; that wasn't an area that I was interested in. 'I will leave you to it then, because I'd rather look at the flower tent and the main ring. Have you got a lift home?' I asked.

'Yeeees', Bill said, stretching back in his chair and putting his hands behind his neck. 'Are you going to desert me now?' He put on his sad voice.

'I certainly am – I've had as much of you as I can stand', I teased. 'I'll catch up with you in a month or so because I'd like to bring some of our group out to see how much damage the badgers do to your corn.'

'You do that, bloody things, people don't realise how much damage . . .'

I got up quickly and touched his arm. 'See you soon, take care' I said, and made a move.

'Oy', Bill's voice bellowed and I looked back, but it was not me he was hollering to. It was someone else's turn to hear about the badgers.

I made the most of my day at the Bath and West Show and stayed to watch the hot air balloons take off from the main ring at the end of the show. It was certainly a spectacle with all the different shapes unfolding as the flames breathed hot air into the slowly unfolding canvases. One day, I shall take a balloon flight. They certainly look exhilarating as the 'can of lager', Michelin man, and even a bunch of carrot-shaped balloons besides the normal ones float effortlessly off into the distance.

Indeed, some of the balloons were still in sight as I wound my way back down the lanes towards home. The heat had gone out of the sun and it was refreshing to drive through such beautiful countryside as we have in Somerset.

On arriving home, Mandy was on late duty until 10 p.m. but it still meant that after 10 there were baby birds needing to be fed every hour until midnight, and the last feed to give the hedgehogs, so I went to the hospital room to make sure that I knew what had to be done before going through to have a coffee with Derek. It was already 9.30 p.m. and Mandy was just clearing up the last few things having fed the baby robins before going to shut up the chickens.

'How are the robins doing?' I questioned as I stood by watching them. Sensing that someone was there, the robins immediately stretched their necks, all four mouths gaping despite the fact that they had only just been fed.

'They're fine', she replied. 'They seem to be the easiest of the fledglings that we care for, don't they?'

I nodded.

Mandy had been with us for nearly ten years. She had come straight from school and had seen Secret World grow from being an open farm to a wildlife rescue centre. As things had changed, she had taken on more responsibility in a supervisory role, but she enjoyed working the evening shift when she could work on her own and not have to worry about anyone else! Tall and slim with dark hair, Mandy was now in her late twenties and yet to have a settled relationship with anyone. I think her strong love of animals meant that men came second.

'Had a good day?' Mandy asked.

'Yes, fine', I replied. 'How about you, has it been busy?'

She smiled. 'Oh, you know, the usual, call-outs just when you don't want them, a lost child just as milking was about to start – but we survived!'

'See you tomorrow then', I said, leaving her to it, and went through the staff room into our flat. The ugly kittens were curled up together on one of the chairs. They had grown, but they were still as black and ugly as when they had arrived!

Derek was in one of the armchairs in the kitchen reading a paper.

'Hi ya', I greeted as I came into the kitchen, making my way to the kettle. 'Coffee?'

'Yes, please. How was the Bath and West?' Derek asked.

'Hot, tiring but good. I met Bill for lunch', I replied, and proceeded to tell him about the 'diet' that he was on.

Putting his coffee by Derek's chair, I placed mine by the other chair and sank into it.

'Once I've done the last feed for the birds and the hedgehogs, I shall be more than ready to go to bed', I sighed, and stretched out for a magazine from the shelf to read while I drank my coffee.

I noticed on the monitor on the kitchen unit, which shows the hospital room, that the lights had gone out in the room. Mandy must have gone home. Another hour before the baby birds would need to be fed again.

Little did I know that it was going to be a very long night . . .

11 o'clock soon came round and it was time to give the robins their next feed. I changed into my old clothes and made my way to the hospital room. I tend to feed late at night as I am not a very good early riser. As soon as I switched the hospital light on the robins trilled with expectation. Feeding one and then the next, they were soon full. Moving further up the tissue in the box each bird passed a faecal sac as a sign that they had fed enough. The parent bird would usually carry this away to keep the nest clean.

'Clean sheets', I said to them as I tore off some fresh kitchen roll and replaced the soiled tissue under them. 'There you go, nice and clean – next feed at midnight.'

Quietly shutting the door, I again went through the staff room and noticed that Mandy had not remembered to put on the outside light by the badger enclosure. So slipping on my denim jacket, I made my way down to the yard. I have never been afraid of walking around our farm at night; some of our girls don't like it, but when Bluebell was alive, I spent a lot of time outside with her. Automatically checking the chicken houses as I passed them to see that their doors were all shut tight, I strolled down to the dairy where the light switch automatically turned on the light that floodlit the yard in front of the enclosure.

I walked on round to see if the cubs were out, and as I walked up to the enclosure Taffy and Meadow heard me coming and came up to the wire to greet me. Kneeling on the wall to talk to them, I was pleased to see that the other cubs, who had run into the tunnels, on hearing my voice, also came to see me.

As I knelt watching them, I suddenly saw, out of the corner of my eye, an adult badger that had come up to the fence further along. I sat very still, hoping to watch it. It slowly made its way towards me. Keeping very still I watched, thinking that as soon as it realised I was there it would run away. By now it was close to my foot. I was not prepared for what happened next.

Without a sound, the badger lunged forward and gripped my shoe. My immediate reaction of kicking him away resulted in both my shoe and sock coming off in his mouth. Without a chance of any further reaction, he was back immediately, grasping me around the front of my foot. Half standing, I viciously kicked him away from me. Unfortunately, as I kicked him away a lot of skin from the front of my foot went with him and blood spurted from my ankle.

As I was holding up my injured leg the badger attacked again, this time at the front of my other foot, locking on to the skin. Pulling my coat off and with nothing else to use, I beat at him with the coat causing him to release my foot and giving me the chance to jump over him. Unfortunately I lost my footing and dropped the coat: within seconds he was back at me and bit me at my waist. All I could use to keep him away was my hands. Skin was torn on my wrists and upper arms. I was doing everything wrong. I was screaming, which initiates any attacking animal to go in and finish it. Because of the wounds to my ankles and wrists there was a lot of blood, which again enticed the badger to go on.

Eventually I grabbed my coat and as the badger came back once more his bite locked on to the coat rather than me. I swung the coat, with badger still attached, away from me and ran towards the house.

Realising I had got away, the badger followed me; seeing him behind me, I climbed on to the tractor. Beside himself with fury at this 'sow badger' who had cubs in his territory and had no right to be there, the badger also climbed on to the tractor. Sobbing in terror and pain, I climbed higher on to the roller bar where it was impossible for him to climb. It was several minutes before he was prepared to admit defeat and ran off in the opposite direction.

Using my right hand to hold the flap of skin that was torn away from my left wrist, I slowly made my way back down the tractor and, minus one shoe, limped back up to the house unaware of just how much blood I had lost.

Climbing up the stairs to the flat, I called to Derek.

'Got a problem,' I called, 'can you get me a flannel?'

Without seeing me, Derek got up from his chair and went into the bathroom to get me a flannel. Meanwhile, I went into the kitchen to the sink to try and make some cleaning-up efforts to my arms.

'Pauline!!', Derek shouted as he returned to the kitchen and saw me standing in a pool of blood around my feet, with me totally unaware of how much blood I was losing, dabbing at the puncture wounds on my arms.

On seeing all the blood, I said, 'Forget the flannel, I think I need an ambulance.' Wrapping tea towels around my wrists I sank into the chair, putting my legs up on a kitchen chair and holding both arms above my head.

I was obviously by now very white and Derek shot downstairs to call an ambulance. Overwhelmed, I closed my eyes only to be shouted at again by Derek when he came back into the kitchen – because he thought I was dead!

Trying to calm him down, I said 'You'll have to ring Debbie, see if she will come and feed the baby hedgehogs . . . and the birds will need feeding again.' All the time I could think of things that needed to be done, I was alright.

Derek rang Debbie and she was on her way. I explained to Derek what had happened and by the time all that was done, the ambulance arrived.

I had been fine coping up until then but once the ambulance arrived I went into shock and they needed to give me oxygen. One of the paramedics went down with Derek to try and ascertain how much blood had been lost, and was very concerned at the amount that they found. Lapsing in and out of consciousness, I can remember being carried downstairs, Derek saying that he would follow on once Debbie had arrived; I also remember briefly staring up at the ceiling of the ambulance as we travelled along and being impressed that I had been given a flashing blue light!

I was terrified that the Press would pick up the story, knowing that they check on a daily basis as to what incidents come in. I could see that if this was reported in the wrong way people would think that a badger would attack a normal person. This is totally untrue. I knew, as soon as the badger had attacked, that the constant marking of the badgers on my feet had resulted in me smelling very strongly of badger. My very stance of kneeling did not give the impression of a human form, and kneeling with cubs in front of me I looked, smelt and was treated exactly in the way that a badger would be in a territory that it didn't belong to. Even after I stood up, the screaming and the blood had already taken this fight into a frenzy and I was as much to blame as the badger. The only people that have ever been bitten by badgers are people involved with the rehabilitation of badgers, and through familiarity have put themselves at risk. An attack like this would never happen in a normal situation, and I could not bear the thought that the Press might, for their own ends, corrupt the story into a sensational piece of fiction.

I had begged and cried so much to the paramedic who was with me about the problems with the Press, that once I had been wheeled into Casualty, the driver patiently came back to me and said that they had put a Press blackout on the incident, much to my relief.

A very shaken Derek arrived – pleased to see me still alive and having left poor old Debbie to do the last feeds and clean up all the blood!

You suddenly realise what these poor doctors and nurses have to put up with late at night in Casualty. They were already waiting for the police to come to evict someone who was drunk and refused to go. And beside dealing with the normal casualties there were two young people in with drugs overdoses, and the nurses were endeavouring to find out what they had taken and when.

I had to wait my turn, and would have been prepared to wait a bit longer had I known how much it was going to hurt when they started to clean me up. Halfway through the nurse said, 'Oh!, I forgot. You can have some gas and air if it will help you with the pain.' Eagerly accepting, I spent the rest of the time on cloud nine. Because they were bite wounds, it was impossible to be stitched and it was thought that, in time, I may have needed plastic surgery on my left foot. But thankfully I was able to go home before dawn broke and it was good to go back to my own bed.

Daily dressings by our local nurse and attention from my own doctor for the next two months eventually saw the healing of all my wounds without the surgery being thought necessary. But it did mean that all the filming for the next few weeks had to be in long-sleeved tops and trousers to cover all my bandages!

Surprisingly, the episode did not affect me with regard to dealing with badger casualties and the cubs. I knew and understood why it had happened. It certainly did not shake my affinity with badgers.

We decided to set a trap to try and catch the badger but it failed, so eventually we did not bother. However, a close eye was kept on the wire and I must admit, my concern for the cubs' safety increased.

I do know that despite our efforts to keep the story from getting out at the time, one of our regular reporters rang to see if there was any news and one of our naive staff sang the whole story out to him. It was only a few months later, when he confided to me that he knew what had happened, that I realised he had been told.

'Why didn't you use the story?' I asked.

'I didn't think it was one that you would have liked released' was his reply. Some reporters do have consciences – for that I was really grateful.

Despite my injuries, I tried to carry on as best I could. As Carey's cubs were well and truly weaned, we moved them over into our new casualty pen building. This building is far from finished but has got some good large pens useful for mixing badgers together, and it is possible to monitor what is going on. A group of three young orphan cubs that had come to us from West Hatch were put in with her.

Moving them in at the beginning of the day when they were all fairly sleepy, we placed them all in the box together and left them in their new surroundings. Carey's cubs were still considerably smaller than the other cubs but, watching them in the evening, they were just as strong and energetic as the others when it came to playing.

Carey accepted the new cubs as her own, and it was a joy to see her cleaning and preening them all and trying to keep order amongst the lively squabbles over the food.

Within a few days Colin was on the phone. We were both very concerned about the numbers of badger cubs coming in.

'I can take Carey and her cubs if you like and put them in an outside pen. We have Glade's group, which is now up to nine, in another pen, but our other two new pens can't be used as they still have no grass in them. It's leaving you holding a lot of cubs seeing as we pass them back to you', said Colin.

'It's not ideal, but we can cope for a while. Linda's got a group of five, then we have six cubs in with Squeak in the observation pen and then groups of five, six, three and four in each of the casualty pens', I replied.

'Next year's going to be better, with our new pens and your new pens, but that isn't helping us this year, is it?' said Colin.

'Well, we can only do our best', I stated.

I arranged for Carey to go down with her cubs the next day to West Hatch, and they were to be the last badgers that were moved on or off our premises for a while – for we were about to have real problems.

It was still difficult, with my injuries, to do all of the cleaning out, so we managed with the help of the girls. But with so many cubs in, it was taking quite a bit of time.

We noticed that soon after two badger cubs had come in to us from another wildlife centre, the cubs in that pen started to have diarrhoea. This was a group of five cubs in all. Taking them all off food, we gave them lectades for 24 hours. By the next day one of the cubs had lost condition tremendously, and as soon as I saw it, I rushed it straight to the vet. Luckily Liz was on duty and I explained the situation. Seeing the condition of the cub, which had literally gone from a healthy-looking cub to a bag of bones in a matter of hours, she agreed with the need to give it an intravenous drip.

I left it in her care, but before I had even returned home, Liz had rung to say that the cub had collapsed and died within minutes of being put on the drip. All the other cubs looked fine and I hoped against hope that we were looking at an isolated incident. By the next morning, two cubs were found dead in a completely different pen where there had been no sign of illness. Placing them into bags, these were taken to the vet for post mortem.

When Liz rang later in the day, my worst fears were about to be realised.

'We don't know what we are looking at at the moment, but the signs are that something very virulent is hitting the cubs. You must make sure that contact between pens is carefully monitored. Consider the casualty area a no-go area for any other animals. Barrier nurse as much as you can. I suggest we cover them all with a blanket antibiotic but if we are looking at a virus, then there is nothing we can do.' Her words stayed with me for the rest of the day.

All staff were prevented from going into the area and I made sure that only I dealt with the cubs. I got the girls to feed and check the cubs in the observation sett in the hope of keeping any infection away.

The next day two more cubs were dead in a different pen, the remaining cubs from the pen where the first one died all started to look unwell, and uptake of food in all the pens went down, showing that some of the cubs were not feeding. With each pen dealt with in turn, using foot baths, and changing overalls and equipment each time, all the cubs were injected with antibiotics.

Three more were dead by the end of the day, all five being sent for post mortem. The results on the previous two were inconclusive. One of the biggest problems that we have always had is that, because of lack of information, there are no measurements we can use for comparison. Nobody knows what the 'normal' blood levels are for a badger – everything is based on the known data for dogs, so it is all guesswork.

Seven more died in a matter of days and still the earlier five cubs' post mortems did not come back with sufficient evidence to pinpoint the problem. I felt totally drained. I was always tired anyway at this time of year, and added to the shock of the attack, this horrendous loss of cubs took its toll. My head felt continually fuzzy; I was so tired but couldn't sleep. I hated the thought of going down to the pens in case I was to find any more dead or dying cubs, and yet the pull to be constantly checking them was always there.

Linda came over one evening just to get some more food to take back for her cubs. She was very careful to keep well away from me and the pens. That evening one of the girls thought that Squeak did not look very well and brought her up to the hospital room. Linda checked her over but she seemed fine, just a little bit quieter than usual, and when Linda took her back, Squeak tucked into her food with all the other cubs.

By the next morning, it was obvious that the concerns for Squeak's health were warranted. She was semi-conscious and Debbie rushed her to the vets where she was immediately put on a drip.

By midday, Liz was back on the phone.

'I think we have got to look at the possibility of this being a parvovirus outbreak. It's still not identified on culture but with the amount of losses, we've got to do something. I want to come through and vaccinate with live vaccine. I've talked this over with the specialists, the problems with shedding (where the bacteria can be passed in urine and faeces which are therefore contagious), but it's the only option open to us now. It may be too late for them, it may save a few – it's the best we can do. I've ordered the vaccine and it should be with us tomorrow. Is it alright to come out late morning tomorrow and we'll go through them?' asked Liz.

'Yes,' I said, 'anything, anything that will give them a chance, I don't think I can stand much more of this.' I was finding it hard to talk without crying. 'What about Squeak?' I asked hesitantly, not daring to hope for it to be good news.

'She's holding her own,' said Liz kindly, 'but she's a long way from being out of the woods. By the way, Gerry (another vet at the practice) is going over to vaccinate Linda's cubs.'

Putting the phone down, I cried. It was the first time I had cried since the attack. I cried for having lost Bluebell, I cried for the pain and the shock of the attack, I cried for losing the cubs – I cried selfishly for me until there were no tears left.

Eventually, I made myself go to the bathroom to wash my face in cold water. Keeping my hands in the cold water in the basin, I stared at my tired, tear-stained face. It can't get worse, tell me, it can't get worse, I whispered to myself.

The phone call first thing the next morning was to make it quite clear that it could. Now Linda had cubs that were unwell. Was it possible, when she had handled Squeak, that she had carried the virus home on her clothes? I tried to be positive. Maybe it was coincidence. Try not to worry, at least Gerry was visiting that day to give advice. Vaccinated, they would have more protection – but a very worried Linda finished the call.

And the next phone call was the vet to say that Squeak had not made it through the night. I felt physically sick. To have lost any of the cubs was heartbreaking but to have lost her, when she meant so much to Caroline and had been entrusted to me for her care, made me feel totally washed-up.

There was no point in putting off the call to let Caroline know about Squeak. I dialled the number, almost willing for there to be nobody there, but Caroline herself was to answer the phone. I explained everything that had happened, the inconclusive post mortems, the number of cubs dying and finally that we had lost Squeak despite Liz's efforts to save her. I could tell that Caroline was crying but instead of blaming me she gave me support. She told me it was beyond my control, that these things happen, and I doubt that she fully appreciated how much those words meant to me.

If ever there is one thing I have learnt from dealing with wildlife, it is the need to admit to your mistakes and to help keep others from making the same mistakes. And when things go wrong, even the strongest of us need sympathy to help us get through the bad times that we all, at one time or another, experience. Derek was there for me too as a husband, but to have other wildlife carers that understand how it hurts made all the difference. It was being able to talk things over with Colin and Sandra at West Hatch, Gill Pearce's unwavering confidence in me, sympathy from Sue Boyes-Korkis of the Wiltshire Wildlife Hospital, not to mention Debbie and Linda at Secret World who are always towers of strength for me, that gave me the courage to go on. So much kindness shown to me by many, many people.

It was a turning point for me, giving me the strength to pull through and to turn the experience into a positive situation. We vaccinated the rest of the cubs and sadly went on to lose another four, but at the end of the season, out of the 42 cubs that came in to us, 18 were lost through the virus, five were lost through other injuries but 19 still went on for release. None of the kitchen crew in the observation sett were lost, despite losing Squeak. Linda, sadly, did go on to lose three of her cubs but all the others survived.

Because of the problems a special group was formed through our charity, called the Bluebell Sett Clinical Studies Group, which has gone on to create a health protocol that we now follow. Cubs are isolated on arrival until they are blood-tested and then grouped into small numbers. Our facilities have improved and our cubs are vaccinated. We organise Badger Veterinary Days to disseminate information to practising vets across the country. We were totally open with what happened, hoping that others would learn from our mistakes.

Only one very well-known wildlife hospital publicly criticised us in a newsletter. From the article it was obvious that they did not have the full facts; it is a pity they did not just pick up the phone and we could have explained everything to them. They implied that the parvo outbreak was caused by close proximity with dogs, whereas we are practically certain we can pinpoint which badger cubs probably brought the infection in with them. Wildlife would be served much better if people involved with their care worked together to bring more knowledge to the subject, rather than picked fault with one another.

I would never wish to live through such a horrendous period in my life again, nor would I wish for anyone else to experience it.

8

Gentle Giant

It is funny how, after a sense of loss, your mind becomes focused and you see things with clarity. Small events bring joy.

A very excited Debbie called up to me one morning: 'Come and see – the harvest mice have had babies!' she shouted.

I followed her down to the Bluebell Sett room where we have a large tank dressed as a corn field. Crouching down, we watched as three minute babies braved it into the big world from the beautiful spherical nest that the mother had woven on the ears of corn. The mother watched with her nose resting on the tiny entrance to the nest, as the youngsters moved up and down the golden stalks. Once at the top, holding tightly with their paws, their prehensile tail, used as a fifth limb, curved round the stem to support them as they surveyed the scene.

'Aren't they gorgeous,' said Debbie, exhilarated; 'they're our first babies in the tank.'

We had hoped that we would get to see the babies. Certainly the mother had been obviously pregnant for quite a few days and all had gone quiet. The male was often seen, as was a much slimmer female, but it was a question of wait and see. Because mice grow so quickly, in order to survive, it was within only ten days from birth that these babies were now out and exploring their surroundings.

Sadly, harvest mice are now becoming quite rare. Again, farming practices of silage-making mean that the long grasses are no longer left to go to seed in the way that they do for hay-making. The constant spraying of corn fields also removes the variety of food sources that used to be available to these tiny mammals and their numbers have declined. Progress in food production demands a heavy price from the livelihood of our wildlife.

I am sure we must have wasted over half an hour, just watching these tiny harvest mice moving around the tank, often jumping nervously when something moved but slowly gaining confidence in their climbing and getting to know the layout of the tank. One tiny baby found the seed pot and proceeded to raid this handy larder of food. Another discovered a mealworm, which it quickly snatched and tried to master climbing a stalk to keep this prize away from the others. Once getting to a distance considered safely away from the others, using its tail and back legs, it balanced, allowing the young mouse to use his front paws to hold the mealworm securely as he quickly devoured it. Clearly harvest mice eat seeds and insects in their diet – fruit as well. Weaning of harvest mice obviously does not take long!

We both became aware that we should be doing other things and started to make a move.

'Seeing that baby reminds me,' said Debbie, 'I must order some more mealworms.' And off she went. In the hospital room we keep a supply of mealworms, which are like shiny caterpillars, as they are a food source for bats, some birds and also hedgehogs. They are useful as a feed for anything that eats insects, giving a variety instead of just using a dry insect mix.

Debbie has always had an interest in bats. She came to us originally as a volunteer many years ago. She was at the time working at a beauty farm – a far cry from our kind of farm! Short, with blonde hair, Debbie is a very attractive young lady, and having worked in hotels before has a very good manner with the general public. When Debbie first came as a volunteer, she said she didn't mind what she did – she just loved animals. One of the first jobs we got her to do when she turned up was to clean the windows on the other side of Reception. The only problem was that she was going to have to go in with a very large white boar and two saddleback sows.

I had my doubts as to whether this pretty young lady was going to be prepared to muck in and cope with the large animals. Gamely she gathered up the window cleaner and cloths and disappeared towards the pigs. Climbing over the gate, in with the pigs, she disappeared. Well, I thought to myself, she handled that OK. But within minutes, she gave out a tremendous scream; smiling to myself, I ran over to see what had happened. Debbie had marched through three very large pigs without batting an eyelid. What was she screaming about? – a little tiny spider up in the corner of the window!

Within a couple of months we were able to offer Debbie the job of manageress, and she worked so hard helping with the staff as well as with the rearing of orphans. It was quite a shock, therefore, six months later when she told us that she and Mike, her partner, had decided to take a year out in Australia. She really did not want to leave her job but Mike was at the age where if they did not do it now, the opportunity would be gone.

We managed to cope for that year without Debbie and kept her job open for her. She and Mike had a wonderful year, working hard to have enough money to tour around, and they managed to see much of the main areas of Australia. But we were very pleased when it was time for her to come back to us. It was ironic that she was now helping to keep our son Simon's job open for him, while he and Nikki also did their year out in Australia, being due back in the autumn.

Once back with us Debbie continued her interest in bats and over the years became friendly with Cherry, a lady who lives in nearby Axbridge and has cared for bats for many years. Cherry had had two noctule bats that were unable to be released, Himmy and Bertha; she used them for educational talks but she was finding it more and more of a responsibility on top of being in full-time employment. So she offered them to Debbie, knowing that Debbie would care for them very well and also that they would be used far more often in talks at our Centre to help people understand a lot more about bats.

Debbie is attached to Himmy and Bertha – 'attached' in more ways than one, as she very often wears them under her sweatshirt where they sleep quite happily! It's only when they 'have a bit of a domestic', as Debbie calls it, and argue over the roosting point under her jumper that you hear the clicking noises and realise that she has got her bats with her. However, she does have a proper box for them when they are not resident with her!

I always smile when she does the talks at schools because Debbie is somewhat well-endowed in the breast section. As she stands in front of the schoolchildren patting the front of her sweatshirt saying 'Guess what I've got under here?' she risks the fact that one of these days, a very forward little child is probably going to tell her!

Because the noctule bats are the larger of our species Debbie is able to show them eating, and they 'click' with excitement as Debbie feeds them with the mealworms so people are able to hear the noises that they can emit, in the same way as they send their sonar signals to help them fly. The children are usually fascinated as they see Himmy and Bertha munching their way through the mealworms, and are even fascinated by the mealworms themselves – you sometimes see the children proudly holding in their hands a mealworm that Debbie has allowed them to have for a while!

Unfortunately, many adults do not like bats, but it is surprising how having the opportunity of seeing them close up and also touching them results in people understanding them much better. Hopefully these people would be more sympathetic if they were to find a roost in their house. Bats are relying more these days on modern houses for their roosts and if you see how tiny the pipistrelle bat is, our smallest bat, it is easy to see how small a hole there needs to be for them to gain access under the eaves of a roof, or even a tile that has just slipped slightly.

Bertha has been looked after for over eight years and is probably the only noctule bat in the country to have lived so long in captivity. As it is unknown how old she was when she was found with a broken wing, we do not know her real age. Despite the wing healing, she has never been able to fly well enough to fend for herself. Himmy joined her only four years ago when he was injured whilst roosting in a tree that was felled. We think that there was probably some brain damage as Debbie describes him as 'a brick short of a load'. However, he enjoys life and is good company for Bertha but again, we do not know his true age so he could be quite old.

One afternoon, a phone call from Mrs Smythe, who lived just down the road at West Huntspill, told us about a baby pipistrelle bat that they had found on their garden path. She explained that they had a roost of bats resident but she did not know what to do. With baby bats, it is always best to try and get them back with their mother but at the moment the little baby was very cold and not looking at all well. Debbie asked Mrs Smythe if she could bring the baby down and she was only too pleased to do so.

I was in Reception with Debbie when the baby bat arrived. It was about five or six days old as it had already turned black (they are usually pink when first born). Even so, it literally was the size of the tip of Debbie's finger. The babies are carried on the front of the mother and can sometimes be dropped accidentally; alternatively, they can be discarded by the mother if she knows that there is something wrong with it, so we were not sure if this was a true orphan or a discarded one.

The most important thing was to warm the baby bat up and already Debbie had a pouch with some soft cotton wool around her neck, into which she placed the tiny baby. With the pouch under her jumper, it would soon become as warm as Debbie's body and we have found in the past that baby bats do much better if they are close to a body and can hear a heartbeat.

There was a chance that if the baby became a little stronger and we were to go back to the house that night, the mother may come back for it, so Debbie and I made arrangements with Mrs Smythe to go up to her house around 10 p.m. when she said that the bats are usually starting to emerge.

Over the next few hours, using a very tiny feeder, Debbie carefully fed the baby bat with lectades and it slowly became stronger. As Mrs Smythe's house was on the main A38 in West Huntspill and Debbie lived in the opposite direction, we arranged to meet at the house later that evening. Debbie took the baby home with her to keep it warm.

The house, when I arrived there, was a very modern one that had been built only five years earlier. The bats had moved in after the third year and were only resident between May and August, so it was obviously a nursery roost. Bats are another species that we do not know an awful lot about, other than that they have separate roosts at different times of the year. Sometimes a roost will consist of purely males, other times a roost will be mixed sexes but will be used only for hibernation. The nursery roost is where just the females gather to have their young.

The breeding cycle of the bat is quite unusual. Some animals have delayed implantation (like the badger) which means they have the capacity to mate at any time but the egg does not implant into the lining of the womb until the female slows down in the winter, which can be several months later. But the bat has delayed fertilisation, which means that once the female has been impregnated with sperm at mating, the sperm and eggs are kept separate within the body until the bat is ready for reproduction to start.

Debbie was already there and standing talking to Mrs Smythe in the garden. It had been a glorious hot sunny day and even though the sun was going down, the evening was very warm. There were plenty of midge flies around for the bats to feed on, and the street lights would attract moths which would be another good food source for them too. As Mrs Smythe took us around to the side of the house, Debbie and I were amazed at the noise from the hundreds of bats all chattering as they clung under the eaves. The timbers running up to the apex of the roof were black with all the tiny bodies of the calling bats, just waiting for the first brave leaders to fly off on their feeding forays.

Debbie quickly took the baby bat from her pouch and placed it as high as she could on the timber-framed lattice work that supported a row of fragrant roses. Small as it was, the tiny baby turned around, lifted its head and appeared to be calling.

The first wave of bats left the roost, circling together before they appeared to divide up and go in other directions. Then after a short period of time it was as if a message passed through them all that it was time to leave, and wave after wave of the bats left the roof in search of food. Soon it was just a few stragglers (probably the late risers) that took to the air. But our baby stayed untouched on the post.

In the past people have even stood by the roost with baby bats on their hands and the mothers have come and picked them up, but this was not to happen to Debbie's little bat. Eric, as he had been named, was put safely back in his pouch. It is always worth a try to get orphans back to their mother, but only if you can be sure that they are with the right mother and are able to survive.

We stayed and chatted for a while to Mrs Smythe and her husband. They had no problems with the bats being there. It was so nice to meet people who cared in that way. What I wouldn't give to have that fantastic spectacle to watch each night from my own garden.

Secretly, I think Debbie was pleased to have her baby bat to look after. She cared for him so well. Within a week another little bat was brought in, found where there was no knowledge of a roost, so Eric was joined by Charlie.

Our local photographer rings on a regular basis to see if there are any animal stories and was keen to come out when he heard about the baby bats. He was even more keen when he arrived and heard that Debbie was keeping them in her bra. Was it possible, he asked, if he could take a picture of Debbie with her top off and the baby bats sitting happily on her bra? Ever keen to obtain money for our charity, Debbie wanted to know how much of a donation he was prepared to give to get the picture! Some bartering went on and a deal was struck, and Debbie bravely removed her top in the front garden for the agreed picture.

This more than made the day of the coach drivers who were inside the tearoom at the time, having coffee while their groups toured the Centre, in full view of what was going on in the front garden. A very attractive picture was the result of this photo shoot, and the photographer was not only able to get it published in the local paper but sold it to the nationals. Debbie in bra with bats was spread across the country, with the ultimate insult when the *Daily Sport* published the picture: typical of the style of this wonderful newspaper, just the bra and bats were shown – they cut Debbie's head off!

A magazine contacted Debbie after seeing the photographs and wanted to write an article on her bats. They offered a nice sum of money as a donation for the charity in return for exclusive rights to the story. They explained to Debbie that a photographer would come down in a couple of weeks to get the pictures to go with the story.

Unfortunately a few days later little Charlie died. It is so upsetting for Debbie when she loses a baby bat as it is still very much a question of luck as to whether they survive or not. Perhaps the milk is not quite right, we really do not know; but little Eric continued to do well and was quite happy snuggled in his pouch.

It was, as promised, a few weeks later that the photographer arrived for pictures for the magazine. He was most concerned when Debbie explained about one of the baby bats having died. The story was about two baby bats, it had all been written up and allocated space for the next issue, and he had been given definite orders for the pictures that were required. This was very serious, he warned; it could well put her payment at risk. Debbie was vexed to know what to do – he definitely wanted a picture of her with two baby bats on her bra. He could do the feeding and the close-up of her face with one, but he had to have the picture with the two.

Inspiration came to Debbie as she remembered that very often, when bats and other small animals die, we keep them in the deep freeze to use for First Aid Wildlife Courses that we have at our Centre to explain how to handle and bandage these creatures. It would be far too stressful to use live animals. So telling the photographer to wait a minute, she sprinted upstairs to have a sort through the deep freeze. Luckily she found a very small dead pipistrelle that, from a distance, would pass as little Charlie.

Meeting up again with the photographer, Debbie explained her way out of the problem, and on commission himself, the photographer was happy to play along with her suggestion. If you ever find a magazine with a story about Debbie and her two baby bats, just take a look at the picture of her in her bra taken slightly from the side. The baby bat nearest should look very healthy, but a close inspection of the baby bat furthest from the camera may lead you to believe that it doesn't look all that well! In fact, because of the hot sun, the frozen bat kept sliding off her bra as the photographer took so long getting the picture. Still, he got his picture and his commission, and thanks to Debbie, the Bluebell Sett charity got their donation!

Early summer is the time for baby hedgehogs and, despite asking people who find them to give their mum the chance to come back for them, there are usually plenty that need hand-feeding. It is now at the beginning and end of the day that our staff arrive or go home complete with a plastic tub, heat pad and small charges to care for, sometimes right through the night. We are very lucky that our staff and volunteers are prepared to take on baby animals, which do so much better with one person caring from them, but it does mean a lot of dedication and time to be given up on their behalf.

It's quite funny to see the girls chatting in the hospital room, discussing whose babies are eating the most, which ones are putting on the most weight and how soon they have started to wean. It is just like an ante-natal clinic with a whole load of broody

It is just like an ante-natal clinic . . .

hens! It doesn't always go down well with their partners – a first taste of noses being put out of joint because a 'baby' is in the house!

Beauty

My next baby was the kind that I always love having. It was a very young roe deer which had been found by the body of its dead mother on the side of the road. As with the badger cubs, we do all the roe kid rearing for our local RSPCA. Russell, the ambulance driver, brought the young deer in to us.

The kitchen cubby-hole again comes into use. Switching on the infra-red light to warm the small frightened animal, I placed him on a fleece and then covered the front with a towel, allowing him to feel secure in a darkened area.

Young roe deer are exquisitely marked with dappled white spots covering their body. Beauty, as I had already named him, tucked his incredibly fine long legs under his body and settled under the heat. His long ears turned like antennae at the least noise and the small shiny nose flared with nervousness. There is a camera in the cubby-hole, so without moving the towel, I was able to see that, for the moment, he was quiet.

At least we knew that this one was in need of care. So often, young roe deer are picked up by concerned members of the public who find them lying up in long grass on their own. And yet this is perfectly natural as the mother only comes back to feed them once or twice a day. The golden rule with wildlife, many of which are left on their own for periods of time by their parents, is this: as long as they are healthy looking, leave them alone and return maybe an hour or so later, just to see if they are still there. If they are, then maybe it is time to consider taking them in and caring for them.

Young fawns are very, very difficult to feed and the cubby-hole works very well in making them feel secure and more confident. I usually leave them until they start to make a peeping noise,which is their call to show that they are hungry. Then very quietly and carefully, I lean over the front cover and try to get them to feed from a syringe with a teat fitted to it. That way I can trickle a small amount of milk just under the lips so that they start to associate me with the source of milk. Once I have gained their confidence and they realise the milk comes from the teat on the syringe, then they start to suck the teat, pulling in the plunger and controlling the flow of milk themselves.

Amazingly Murray, our dog, is a great help with the deer. Despite his size, the fawns seem to take to him and allow him to clean them. This in turn stimulates them to feed. There have been several occasions when I do not think young deer brought in to us would have survived if it had not been for him helping. It's funny – everyone has different ideas and I have heard people being very critical of involving dogs with deer, as they believe that the deer grow up trusting dogs. I can honestly say that it has never been a problem for us and as they are usually weaned and gone from us within three months, perhaps in such a short period it does not get instilled into them.

That evening Beauty still had not made any noise and the scratching on the door of the flat told me that Murray wanted to come in. Our dogs have a strict routine, totally arranged by themselves. 8 a.m. sharp and both Murray and Barney want to go downstairs. The first shift of the staff are due in and breakfast will soon be served to both of them in the backhouse. Barney, now nearly 16 years old, then usually retires to the staff room to wait for coffee break when the staff often have interesting snacks to share. Murray, meanwhile, will follow Sarah or Ellie, depending on who is supervisor, around the farm. He also joins the staff at coffee time.

Lunchtime is a good time, as far as they are both concerned, to sweep the play areas and gardens for anyone eating packed lunches, any remains that may have been left behind – and if all else fails, there is always the staff room to fall back on.

This is usually enough exercise as far as Barney is concerned, and he will usually snooze back up in the staff room until teatime. Meanwhile, Murray believes that he has a busy afternoon ahead of him keeping up with the staff doing odd jobs, before he is ultimately required to bring the cows in at 4 p.m. If he only knew how the girls often try to sneak down there without him he would be dreadfully hurt, but he really is quite useless, often barking just at the wrong time, resulting in the cow or calf hurtling in the opposite direction to the one required, to the moans of 'oh, Murray!' ringing in his ears. He still hasn't worked out that this is not a compliment.

Once teatime has arrived and the dogs and cats are all fed and all the bowls collected up, there is no chance of any more food in this area of the farm and it's time to make their way up to the flat where, at some time or other, tea will be prepared and there is always the chance of a morsel or two.

He is really quite useless at herding cows . . .

146

You have probably realised by now that I am under no illusions as to the loyalty of our dogs, both being totally stomach-driven – although I wouldn't change them for the world!

Letting Murray in through the door, he walked into the kitchen. Sensing a newcomer in the cubby-hole, he pushed the towel to one side with his nose and looked in. Beauty immediately stood up and walked forward to Murray, peeping. Using his big pink tongue, Murray licked the fawn's tiny head. Quickly mixing some milk, I bent down next to Murray and dribbled some milk slowly into the deer's mouth. Beauty licked his lips. I repeated the small amount of milk in his mouth and again he licked his lips. Unsure, he peeped at me and then, folding his front legs, he lay down again under the heat.

I was quite happy with that. Beauty had not panicked and just the fact that he had licked his lips showed that he was feeling secure. Still leaving the towel in place, it gave Beauty the chance to get used to the noise in the kitchen without any movements that may frighten him. Murray lazily made his way to one of the armchairs and sat down. Nothing in this kitchen would surprise him, from badger cubs to play with, to baby rabbits to nurse between his paws, owls sitting on his head and young deer, he's seen it all before. His size belies his nature – Murray is a real gentle giant.

I had cooked Derek's tea and cleared up, with Derek having gone back over to the office to sort out the banking and the wages, before the next lot of peeping could be heard from the cubby-hole. Murray immediately got down from the chair and poked his head over the towel to look at the fawn. His tail wagged as Beauty nuzzled his face. With fresh milk prepared, I filled the syringe and offered the teat to Beauty. Sniffing at the teat, Beauty curled his tongue around the end and sucked briefly, enough to take just 10 mls, and then he stopped.

He was still unsure. Hunger was making him brave but everything was very strange. Moving away from me, Beauty turned nearer to Murray, confident while Murray cleaned his face. Murray's tongue cleaned down his back and then started to clean round his tail. This immediately made Beauty lick his lips and I quickly slid the teat back in his mouth and he sucked strongly at it, quickly emptying the 20 ml syringe.

Refilling the syringe, as Murray continued to clean, I managed to get the teat back into Beauty's mouth and again he sucked and emptied the syringe. Then sniffing the fleece, Beauty again settled in the corner.

'Well done, Murray', I said to him as he made his way back to the chair. 'You're very useful sometimes', I teased, stroking his big head.

There was no one on duty that evening so the time soon went by. I fed some young hedgehogs left in my care and topped up some young seagull chicks with fresh fish before going out to put the food in with the cubs down in the casualty pens. The parvo crisis was well and truly over and, although still saddened by the loss of those cubs, it was good to see that the surviving ones were doing well.

It was time for many releases. Carey with her new family were to be released in the South-West, so the rest of our cubs would be moving down to West Hatch in the next few weeks. From there, Taffy and his crew were due to go to Norfolk. His release was to be filmed for 'Nature Detectives' and I was looking forward to going and actually seeing where their new home would be. We were going to add another couple of female cubs to balance up the sexes prior to their going for release, but that would be done at West Hatch as they were tattooed and blood-tested.

Finally, I would be going to see Glade's group going to their new home in Suffolk, which would mean so much to me. This special release was going to be filmed by Mike Gunton for 'Back to the Wild'.

Having switched on the outside light by the enclosure, I still checked the fence, as I did most evenings. The boar badger was still around but we hadn't actually seen him. Having put the food in the enclosure, I marvelled at how quickly the cubs had grown. Taffy and Meadow were almost young adults now, and surprisingly there was little difference between David, Eric, Ebony or Barley, even though the last two had been so small when they had come in.

It seemed a lot longer than just a few weeks ago that I had my argument with the boar badger. Most of my wounds were nearly healed and only one foot was still needing to be bandaged. The light was starting to fade despite the long evenings as I made my way through the play areas and then along by the poultry pens, shutting each of the hen houses as I went. How different the place must be from when it was a large dairy farm in the early part of the twentieth century, busy making cheese and cider. They employed over thirty people in those days as well as having a resident cheese-maker.

I suppose, if you think about it, we employ over thirty people now, albeit many in a part-time capacity. There are animal carers, cleaners, office staff, tearoom and shop assistants, gardeners and maintenance staff. We've practically come full circle, although now there are all manner of animals, theatre, Visitor Centre, play areas, casualty pens, tearooms, shop, etc., etc. Certainly a 'different' kind of farm.

Derek managed to get back to the kitchen before me, and I caught him making coffee.

'Well done,' I said, 'can I have one too?'

'Yes', he said, reaching for another cup. 'Nearly done?'

'Yep, just one more feed of hedgehogs and then the deer and I'm through', I replied.

'How is the deer?' asked Derek as he moved towards the fridge to get the milk.

'He's taken some, you know how good Murray is with them', I replied.

Derek smiled. Picking up his cup of coffee and the paper he made his way out of the kitchen. 'Well, I'm going to read the newspaper in the front room and then I'm off to bed', he said.

'I won't be long', I said, and made my way to the hospital room.

I love this time at night. No telephone ringing. No one wanting to ask me anything. A chance to sit quietly and feed some baby animals, something which, apart from deer and badger cubs, I seem to do less and less, partly because I have so much else to do but partly because other people take an interest and want to do the work. It was a small family of four hedgehogs that needed to be fed. They were nearly at the point of weaning. They were Ellie's babies but she was away for the weekend and I had promised to take care of them.

Ellie had looked after them well and they were really quite podgy. First I had to get the equipment out of the sterilising unit and mix up the milk. Pulling the chair over to the side of the unit, I draped a towel across my lap. Each baby was lifted in turn, first to toilet with a damp tissue and then to feed with a 1 ml syringe with a small teat on the end. As soon as one baby was missing from the tub, the others called expectantly waiting for their feed.

149

Their call is a shrill squeak that one could almost mistake for a bird.

The young hedgehogs' eyes were open and it would not be long before they would be able to curl into a ball. Once they were all fed and changed on to a clean towel they slept like all young babies once their tummies are full. Two were lying on their sides, but the other two were making the most of the warmth from the heat lamp and were laid on their fronts with their back legs stretched right out.

With the final clearing up done, I switched out the light and only the red glow from the lamps illuminated the room. These were for the young bats that Debbie was caring for, that were hanging on soft material in the bat cage exercising their wings, building up muscles for when it would be time to fly. Tucking their heads under their extended wings they preened the webbing, keeping it all in good order. In the tub next to the bat cage, an adult long-eared bat was tucking into his supper of mealworms conveniently laid out in a dish for him – the hotel service being much appreciated while he convalesced his torn wing. Other than that, all the residents were quiet and most were asleep.

Passing through the staff room, I looked out towards the badger enclosure. All was quiet there too. Both Barney and Murray were asleep in the armchairs in the kitchen as I returned. Mixing up the last milk feed of the day for the deer, I looked across at Murray. He was sound asleep, legs twitching as he dreamed. Rather than disturb him I tried to feed Beauty without his help. As soon as I knelt by the cubby-hole Beauty got up and came over to me. Licking his lips, he searched for the teat and on finding it, soon emptied the syringe.

'You're a good boy', I murmured, as I refilled the syringe.

Beauty took his fill. I was so thankful. In the past, occasionally we have lost youngsters just through refusing to feed, and it really put my mind at rest to know that this one was going to be alright.

It was my time for bed, and switching out the kitchen light left another room in the red glow of the lamp shining from the cubby-hole. Beauty sat quietly chewing his cud. Murray dreamed on and Barney, bless him, snored away.

Within a couple of days, it was possible to leave the front of the cubby-hole off. Beauty would lie up in this area, but as his confidence grew he would charge up and down the hall. If I was

OUNG LIVES - HELLO YOU!

TAKING A FREE RIDE - A BIT SLOW THOUGH!

TEDDY THE FALLOW - MY SHADOW

SO TINY, SO PERFECT, YOUNG ROE DEER

BEAUTY SHARING AN EVENING WALK

BILL GROVES IN HIS CORN FIELD

ELECTRIC FENCING CONTAINING RELEASED CUBS

COLIN SEDDON

NSIDE THE ARTIFICIAL SETT IN THE GRASS ENCLOSURE

Colin Seddon

NEARLY OUTSIDE THE ARTIFICIAL SETT

Colin Seddon

NEW HOME DUG THEMSELVES, FREEDOM AT LAST

NIKKI, SO NATURAL
WITH THE BABIES

SIMON, PRESS AGENT FOR A WALLABY

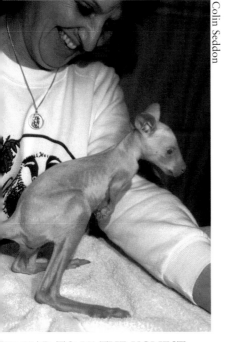

Colin Seddon

Richard Austin

HE HAD TO BE THE UGLIEST
BABY EVER!

INSIDE A MAKESHIFT POUCH,
MR WOO PEERS OUT

"MR WOO"

Jason Venus

OUTSIDE THE POUCH - I'M A BIG BOY NOW!

Jason Venus

NIKKI AND MR WOO -
CUPBOARD (RUCKSACK?)
LOVE!

MR WOO, HANDSOME DEVIL NOW

ON THE MOVE!

working in my office, he would come and lie at my feet. Eventually we shared walks in the garden and out into the homeground. The only concern with taking him for a walk was that I had to be on my own. If any other people were around then he would shy away and become very scared.

It was a couple of weeks later that I came up to the flat just after we had closed and found the front door open – not that that was anything unusual with people always going in and out. I went into the kitchen and noticed that Beauty was not in the cubby-hole, which did not unduly worry me as he often lay up in my office. But on checking there, he was not to be found. Methodically going through every room, I looked everywhere for him. Under the bed, in cupboards, behind chairs – nothing. Knowing the door had been left open, I panicked and went into the garden looking behind greenery, searching through the flower beds.

Tania was on a late shift, saw me searching and came out to see if she could help.

'What have you lost?' she asked.

'I can't find Beauty', I said, running my hand through my hair. 'The front door of the flat was open, but I wouldn't have thought he would go down the stairs. But I suppose there's a chance that he would follow Murray.'

We both continued to search. Derek arrived home and he also began to help. He could see how upset I was.

'It's my fault', I started. 'I should have dropped the latch on the door.'

'It's the fault of whoever left the door open,' he replied, 'and anyway, we'll find him' he assured me.

But I knew that Beauty would never show his face to anyone except me, and looking would, in a way, drive him further into the undergrowth, if indeed he was out here.

I went back into the house and went through the flat again: room by room, every place I thought he could physically get into. By this time Tania had rung Debbie to see if she had seen Beauty as she had been out to a talk at a school in the afternoon and had brought all the equipment back up to the flat before she went home. Tania thought Debbie might have seen him, and at least then we would know roughly how long he had been missing.

Debbie had not seen him when she had come up to the flat and she was sure that she had closed the door when she left. Equally upset, she drove over to assist in the search. We all checked round the garden and out to where I usually walked with Beauty – nothing. Debbie came back up to the flat with me and we again went from room to room thinking of where he could be. By this time we were both in tears. It was starting to get dark. Debbie went down to continue looking in the garden with Derek. Tania had had to go on with seeing to the orphans and locking up the chickens.

I went along to my office and just stood there completely mystified. I glanced round at my desk, the wardrobe, the cupboard where the projector and slides were kept – and noticed the small four-inch gap between the side of the cupboard and the wall, where we slid the screen and projector table. Getting a torch, I looked down the side but the stand and screen were all I could see. But I could see that the cupboard did not go right to the wall at the back, and climbing on a chair, I shone the torch down the back of the cupboard to see a perfectly calm roe deer fawn chewing its cud and looking up at me.

What had happened was that Beauty, while Debbie had the stand and screen out for the talk, had lain down beside the cupboard. Debbie had come back, and without looking, had pushed the screen and table down the side of the cupboard not realising that Beauty was there. All Beauty had done was to walk on behind the cupboard as Debbie had pushed the equipment in.

A very joyful Pauline went down to tell everyone that I had found him! I didn't mind that we had all wasted nearly four hours looking for him, or that we had to practically take my office apart to get at him – he was safe and that was all that mattered. Debbie and Tania shared my joy. Derek could have happily sat down to venison pie!

Something else was found a few days later which was really exciting. A caretaker from Hugh Sexey's school at nearby Mark came in with a bat that he had had to catch during the night. Somehow or other it had got into the school and had set all the burglar alarms off. So in the middle of the night this poor man had spent quite a bit of time pursuing this animal, charging from one class to another until he managed to catch it. Debbie went to meet him and he explained that there was a roost of bats in their cellar, but they had never bothered very much about it.

Debbie explained that it was just as well to bring it in to have it checked, but if it was healthy (and judging by the time it took to catch it – it certainly sounded so!), the best thing to do would be to take it back that evening and let it go. Carefully sliding her hand into the box, Debbie cupped it in her hands and brought it out to have a look at it.

She was amazed to see that it was a greater horseshoe bat, one of the rarest species that we have in this country. Many, many ardent bat workers have never had the privilege of seeing a live one. It had a ring on its wing so it was one that was being monitored, so once she had checked it over, she returned it safely to the box. (There is a lesser horseshoe bat which is not quite so rare.)

It was necessary to contact the local bat group to find out what needed to be done and within a very short period of time a licensed bat worker called to collect it. It was important that the bat was handled very carefully. From the markings on the ring they were able to tell that this bat was fitted with the ring in 1984 in Cheddar, which is about twenty miles away from us. It was an adult at this stage so the actual age of the bat was unknown. The bat had been found again in Axbridge, a village adjoining Cheddar, in 1990 and now, six years on, it had been found again.

The greater horseshoe bat was once common in the southern part of Britain, but now it has become so scarce that it is believed that this species could be in danger of extinction. Loss of habitat, as with other bat species, has had much to do with their decline. They need places rich in insects, such as hedges, ponds and old grassland.

I can remember an article in our local paper, written by a friend of mine, that was headed 'Eat meat, save a bat!' Michael Woods, the author, was to explain that if we were to stop eating meat the cow would disappear, and as the dungs from these animals are a very rich food source for the dung beetle, a major item in the greater horseshoe bat diet, it would have grave repercussions for the survival of this animal. So many things are done these days without thinking through the true effect on the total environment.

Most bats fold their wings against the side of their bodies when they are not flying, but the horseshoe bat drapes the wings around the body creating a cloak. They are therefore unable to crawl and need to find roosts such that they can fly straight to the perching areas, whereas other breeds can crawl through small gaps to obtain access to where they sleep.

The other major difference with these bats is the way that they find their way around. Other bats have a pointed lobe, like an inner ear, called the tragus which picks up the high-pitched sounds that they make through their mouths in order to echo-locate. But the horseshoe bat emits the sound through its nose, hence the nose leaf that makes it so distinctive from other bats, and this noise is then directed back to a cone-shaped trumpet on the snout. (Sort of like a 'high class' bat!) I find bats fascinating creatures – like the badger – still so much to find out about them!

Sadly Jason Venus, who had been coming over to our Centre throughout the season to film a lot of our work, missed this bit of excitement. Still, there was much that he had captured on film ready to make our own video which we hoped to retail. He had filmed the badger cubs, foxes and many orphans, together with visitors and demonstrations. But he had never been around when we had been called out to a road casualty. Having been involved with filming for television, I was beginning to understand all the footage that is required, from different angles, and the time needed to achieve an item. And I truly believe that if an incident such as an accident is filmed, then the priorities (which should be the injured animal) get confused.

We have tried on occasions to take cameras with us, to film call-outs, but we always end up by saying, forget the camera, let's just get on with this in order to deal with the situation as quickly and sympathetically as possible. I therefore had this wonderful idea that we could mock up a call-out to a road traffic accident where a badger had been run over.

We decided to use the body of a badger that we had in the deep freeze and so got it out the previous day to defrost ready for the 'accident'. Jason arrived at lunchtime complete with camera and director's board (he's such a poser!) and we surveyed the site for this accident. Not wishing to go too far, we used our lane outside. The story went that the badger had been run over and we had been called out by the driver. We needed a car, so I borrowed my father's car who at the time was busy working on Reception.

Then we needed a driver, so my poor mother who is not a driver (!) had to be the nasty person who had done the deed. We fetched the badger to lay on the road – it was unfortunately still a little frozen and had a somewhat stiff expression on its face. But the camera can lie! And with clever camera work, Jason achieved our arrival on the scene – me telling my mother not to worry, she could not have helped running over this poor frozen badger and, with great care, us managing to get the badger into the cage without it biting us. You then see us driving off hurriedly to the vet to try and get the best possible veterinary attention for this injured and severely hypothermic badger.

Liz, our vet, was prepared to help us, and when we arrived with our dead badger she had got out some old x-rays of a badger with a fractured spine. By now we were really getting into the swing of things and acting was our second nature! The storyline was for the injured badger to be examined on the table. This was the first hiccup, as still slightly frozen, the badger would not lie flat on the table and its head was raised a few inches. So we tucked a towel under its head to give the appearance of it 'resting' its head.

We solemnly discussed the injuries that Liz had found and she pointed to the x-rays that had supposedly been taken. 'Sadly he was too ill', she started to say . . . and a slight snigger from the cameraman made it necessary to do a second take.

Trying again, with serious faces, Liz started again. 'Sadly he is too ill, and it is obvious from the x-rays that he would never be able to survive', she said softly; 'I really think that the kindest thing to do will be to put him to sleep while he is still . . .'

The word we were waiting for was 'anaesthetised' but Liz came out with 'while he's still frozen'.

We all dissolved into laughter. 'Oh, I'm so sorry,' said Liz, putting her hand up to her mouth, 'I didn't mean to say that.'

Do you think, even when Liz said the right words, that we could get past that bit without laughing? It took us ages and endless takes!

If you've watched the video, I'm sorry to have dispelled your impression. I've had people come up to me and tell me how it made them cry, and that's what it was meant to do. It may not have happened exactly there as you saw it, but we experience it in real life time and time again. Laugh at it as we did when we were acting – we cry like you when it happens in real life.

9

Cut!

Beauty continued to be my companion but with his increasing intake of goat mixture and browse, I began to realise that he was more than capable of fending for himself with better outside conditions. Now lapping, Beauty no longer needed bottle-feeding and so would be much happier down with Colin at West Hatch, where they already had another young weaned roe deer in the paddocks.

The transporting down is always very difficult as the best thing to do is to put them in a box and cover it so that it is nice and dark. The very act of catching Beauty to put him in the box made me feel that I was betraying him – his trust had allowed me to hold him in the first place and then I had bundled him in a container.

Still, he remained very quiet and Debbie helped me carry the box to the car in the courtyard.

'You're going to miss him, aren't you?' Debbie said, as we closed the back of the car.

I nodded, without saying anything. It's at times like this that it is better to think that they are going to have much more space and be able to graze properly than to think too much of sentimentality.

The run down to West Hatch was easy and Colin, already notified that I was on my way, was ready for me as soon as I got there so that Beauty did not have to stay in the box any longer than necessary.

Carrying the box down the grassy pathway through the paddocks, I could see that Beauty was going to be much happier here with all this space.

'Oh! you've got two roe', I said to Colin as I could see the fleeting forms running off into the long grass.

'Yes,' said Colin, 'another one came a couple of days ago.'

Opening the gates to the enclosure, it was just possible to make out the twitching ears of the other two deer, well camouflaged in the long grass but watching what was going on.

We made our way to a wooden shed, which Beauty would go into to start with. This was surrounded by an area within the paddock fenced with plastic windbreak just to contain him in a smaller pen while he got used to the new routine.

As I was quietly placing the box inside the shed, Colin went out to leave me alone so that I could let Beauty out. Opening the door, I was relieved to see that he was lying down quite calmly inside. There is always the danger of them damaging their fine legs in transit, which is a constant worry. Beauty was fairly quick in coming out of the box to see his new surroundings. He peeped, calling to me for reassurance. Soothing him, I talked quietly and slowly opened the bottom half-door out into the small enclosure and he hesitantly walked out into the afternoon sunshine.

The other deer were quite visible now; they had come to the edge of the long grass, aware that a newcomer had arrived. But they were not prepared to leave the safety of the overgrown cover to see any more. Beauty made a couple of bounds through the grass and then started to chew the green shoots.

While he was busy eating, I slipped out of the pen. But it was not long before Beauty realised I had gone. I could hear a horrible screaming sound as he called in panic at being left alone, and I had to suppress every wish to go back to him. He was running along the edge of the mesh trying to find me, so I moved away quicker knowing that within a short while he would concede that I had gone.

'Come and have a look at Carey', Colin said. He could see that I was getting upset. Taking me towards an enclosure further away, he unlocked the wire door and let me through. The terrible noise of Beauty panicking had stopped already and I knew that come tomorrow, out with the other deer, he would have forgotten all about me.

Walking over to the artificial sett in the centre of the paddock, Colin lifted the lid. Black and white heads lifted at the sudden beams of light that entered their dark chamber.

Carey was easy to recognise with her chewed ears and scarred nose, but all the six cubs were the same size and really healthy. I was astonished that from being smaller all through the start of their life, Carey's own cubs had caught up with the other three and they all looked really, really healthy.

'They look really great', I said to Colin. 'When do they go?'

'Carey goes in the next couple of days and then, of course, next week is Glade's journey to his new home. Has Mike Gunton from the BBC been in touch?' asked Colin.

I nodded. 'The strawberry blond', I joked. 'What's this all about an aeroplane and flying the badgers up there?'

'Well, it makes the storyline more interesting, but they are only taking one up by plane – we've got to take the others up by van and meet them there, pretending that all the cubs were flown up', laughed Colin.

'Oh!, so much for the air flight I was hoping for', I quipped.

'Ahh!' taunted Colin, 'play your cards right and you might get a flight home.'

With spirits lifted, I made my way home. The kitchen seemed empty with Beauty not there, but in my heart I knew he was better off where he could roam freely. Eventually, once the autumn had come, because there are roe around West Hatch Centre, Colin would leave the gates on the enclosure open and the deer would gradually make their way to the woods behind and freedom.

Glade's Journey

The chance to see the release the next week was good too, as it is the final stage of caring for the cubs and makes all the hard work worthwhile. So I was really looking forward to it – air flight or not!

The journey to Suffolk for the release the following week called for an early start and it was hard to find a tremendous amount of enthusiasm as I turned in to the gates of West Hatch at 4 o'clock in the morning. Glade, Poppy and Flora, together with the other five cubs, had been brought into the care pens two days earlier from their outside enclosure. This was to give them their last blood test and a complete health check prior to going for release. Now already boxed in travel cases in the van, they were ready for their journey.

One cub was staying behind to be taken to the airport for his flight with the film crew. But it was only going to take them just over half an hour to get to Suffolk, whereas we had a four- to five-hour journey ahead of us. Climbing up into the front of the van, I looked forward to a restful drive up there. No point in offering to drive as Colin is one of those sad males who won't sit in a car with a woman driving, so I was quite happy to let him get on with it.

There was a bit of scratching going on in the back but most of the cases were quiet.

'I can tell you who's making all the noise', said Colin as we went along.

'Glade?' I guessed.

'Yes', said Colin. 'I still have my doubts about him being too tame, but seeing as they are going to a site that Margaret and Martin (members of the Suffolk Badger Group) are monitoring, and they've been doing it for years, I was happy to leave the final decision to them. If he comes out during the day or comes up to them, he'll have to come back.'

I knew what that meant, because if a badger is too tame for release the answer is usually to put them down. I went quiet.

'Don't worry,' said Colin, looking across at me, 'given new surroundings again, I'm sure he'll be fine. I wouldn't have taken it this far if I hadn't thought there was a good chance of him making it.'

Why is it that every time, for whatever reason, I get up early and see the dawn break, I always think to myself – I should do this more often. The cloud formation accentuated the beautiful colours as morning unfolded as we sped through the open countryside. (I know why really, because when I am in bed I open my eyes, look at the clock and decide that it's nicer to stay in bed – I'm just not an early person. Still, I used to get up every morning at 5.30 when I worked as a dairymaid when I left school and never thought anything of it . . . must be getting old!)

One hour passed and then two, and we stopped briefly for a coffee and checked our charges who all seemed to have gone to sleep. We approached the dreaded M25. Being still the early hours of the morning, the roads were not congested and we travelled the circular route eventually picking up the A12 and back into countryside.

Every so often we checked the carrying cases through the window behind us in the back of the van. Suddenly I thought I heard a noise behind me and looked through the window to see if all was well. A black and white face stared back at me, and if he had had the ability, I'm sure he would have waved.

'Em, Colin,' I pointed, 'there's a badger out in the back.'

'A what!' Colin said, braking carefully and pulling the van up to a halt. 'I don't believe it', he said as we watched the badger casually walk over all the cases, sniffing here and sniffing there. 'You don't think that's . . .'

'Glade,' I finished for him, 'well, it looks very much like him and just the typical thing he would go and do. I've never had a cub that could cause so much trouble . . .'

A black and white face stared back at me . . .

Getting out of the van, we both peered through the back door windows to survey the scene.

'You'd better shut me in there, and I'll try and get him back in the cage', said Colin.

Great idea, I thought, I wasn't absolutely sure that it was Glade and if someone else was prepared to risk getting bitten, I was all for that.

Of course, I was full of advice and encouragement once I'd slammed the door behind him after Colin climbed in, with the door held open ever so slightly just so that he could get in. Glade did three circuits of the back with Colin in hot pursuit until he gave in, as Colin ever so gently (!) persuaded him to go back in his box.

'I shall be glad to see the back of that animal', said Colin as he climbed back in the van. Sometimes he sounds just like Derek – their love of animals just *shines* through!

The rest of the journey was uneventful and we arrived at the airport just in time to see the plane landing and everyone climbing off fresh as a daisy, with us jaded after our long drive. The last cub was filmed being offloaded into the van as if everyone else had come the same way, and we all set off to the release site which was just half an hour away.

We came to a narrow track leading up through fields of corn and pasture land. There were hardly any houses in sight; it was an area very rarely frequented other than by the landowners.

The site was a beautiful wooded site and the Suffolk Badger Group had electric-fenced off a really large area that was to be the badger cubs' new home. It had been surveyed the year before to check that there were no badgers living there, and then the group members had needed to check that the area would support the new family of badgers for food and make sure that the landowners (and adjoining landowners) were happy to have them released on their land. Straw bales had been set up as a temporary home but near to that was an old rabbit warren, and no doubt the cubs would soon dig into these and make their own sett to live in.

Margaret and Martin were there to meet us, busy checking all the final details, making sure that the fence was erected properly and that the cubs would be safe. Parking the van under the shelter of the large oak trees, the film crew started to get the cameras and equipment in place ready to film the badgers going into their new home. It gave me a chance to go for a short walk and pick up some more cones, here and there, to remind me of yet another home for my kitchen crew.

Ready at last, the cameras rolled, filming the wooden cases being unloaded and being carried down the wooded banks to where the straw home had been set up. This in itself is no mean task as by now the badgers are quite heavy, and with two in a box, even with poles as handles, they are quite difficult to carry too far.

You're not a happy chappy when you have manoeuvred the boxes down a fairly steep bank only to hear that little voice say: 'Yes, good, but can we just do that once more as I missed you moving round to the side.' But eventually, each case was opened and the badger cubs ran into the artificial sett; the front was then blocked with straw just to discourage them from coming out during the day. Colin and I were interviewed about how we felt seeing them go to their new home.

Then Martin and Colin were interviewed and Colin explained how it would now be the badger group's responsibility to give the cubs fresh water and food in their fenced-off enclosure for five or six weeks to give them the chance to settle in their new area. Then the electric fence would be taken down and it was hoped that the family would stay there for the rest of their lives. Certainly the badger group would monitor the cubs, and report as to the success of the release and whether the group went on to breed and establish themselves.

The cameraman was left behind as he was to sit quietly and hopefully film them emerging for their first night of freedom. Colin sadly (!) had to drive the van home – but I got the chance to fly back with the rest of the crew. On reaching the small airport, which was only grass, my excitement ebbed as I started to consider just how small these little hired planes looked. Ours was actually larger than most of them 'parked' in the field, but still lacked obvious substance.

We climbed into the body of the plane and strapped ourselves to our seats as the engines roared into life and the plane started to turn to take full advantage of the length of the field.

Leaning forward, Mike Gunton called out to me, 'I'll tell you what the pilot said in a minute!' And then all possibility of talking ceased as the engines roared and we bumped our way along the uneven grass. Seconds before we appeared to be heading for the hedge, our heads were forced into the backs of the seats as the plane veered up into the sky. Levelling out, the engine roar became quieter and the plane, finding its course, sped effortlessly towards its destination.

Mike Gunton, smiling, leaned over. 'The pilot wasn't sure if the field was going to be long enough!' Grateful, I said to him, 'I'm glad you left telling me that until now!'

It was a brilliant flight; being a small plane it takes a lower flight path and the views were tremendous. And having got up in the air – I felt quite sorry for poor Colin driving all the way home!

News about the release two days later was that the cubs had dug a new home in the rabbit warren the very next night, using the straw bales of the artificial sett for bedding. This was really good news as the cubs were far more likely to live permanently in a home that they had dug for themselves. All the cubs had been out exploring on the first night and the cameraman had got some really good footage.

When Martin went up the following day, just before it got dark, to put fresh water and food out for them, none of the cubs came out of the sett. Maybe Glade was going to be alright after all.

Within a few days, I was to get another orphan deer sent to me from the RSPCA, but it was not the usual roe deer. For the first time ever, I was to rear a fallow. It was an unusual colour too. On opening the cardboard carrier, a very angular face appeared; and I could see that the whole of the animal was a deep chocolate brown. Whereas the fawns were usually a chestnut reddish colour with white spots, this one had ginger spots. I placed her in the cubby-hole.

It seems unkind to say it, but she wasn't as pretty as a roe and although she settled on the fleece, she constantly called: not a little peeping noise but a constant 'eea, eea, eea' which was eventually to nearly drive me daft. Reading up about the fallow, I was to find that most wild herds have lived for hundreds of years in ancient forests such as the New Forest, Epping Forest and the Forest of Dean. They are also a species very often favoured for stately homes. Many have escaped so there are several small feral groups around.

The males have the beautiful palmate antlers distinctive to this breed. Most fawns are born in mid-June but late births sometimes occur (hence ours in August). The explanation of the constant calling was that, unlike the roe who are left to lie up in places while the mother feeds, the fallow wander with their mothers. Teddy, as she was to become known, was to be my little shadow and if I wasn't there she would be Derek's little shadow. And Derek didn't like having a little shadow.

'Why does she keep crying!' he commented exasperatedly, when I returned from doing something outside. 'She's in the blasted room with me and she's still bleating.' Teddy ran up to me as I walked into the room. I stroked her head. 'She just wants you to talk to her', I said, turning her nose towards my face as I bent down to her. 'You just want Daddy to talk to you, diddums', I said in a silly voice, making my way back to the kitchen.

Derek shook the newspaper he was reading and disappeared behind it. Teddy blew down her nose in a snort, and pranced beside me as we went down the corridor, her tail in the air and a look of disgust on her face. She certainly did not need 'Daddy' now that 'Mummy' was here. It did take a bit of getting used to: whatever I was doing as I went from one room to another, she would follow me so closely that if I went just to put something down in a room, we'd bump into each other as I came back out again!

We had some more unusual babies that month. Luckily it was an evening when Sarah was doing a late duty and someone rang to say that their cat had brought in two baby ferrets. They still had their eyes closed and they really didn't know what to do with them. Could they bring them in to us?

Intrigued, we said yes, it was no problem. It would be unusual to find baby ferrets in the wild. We have over twenty ferrets at our Centre – all ones that have been rescued from people's gardens. They are either lost pets or ones that have been left down rabbit warrens when they have been used for ferreting. They never seem capable of surviving in the wild and soon look for human contact for a supply of food.

It was a young couple that brought the two babies in. They had wrapped them in a soft scarf in a shoe box. We all peered into the box, the young couple being as intrigued as we were as to the true identity of the youngsters. They were a light brown colour with a white belly going right up to under their chin, both very similar to each other. Although only four or five inches long, their slim elongated bodies made it quite clear that they belonged to the ferret family. But they weren't ferrets. They were either weasels or stoats. The stoat is the larger of the two species but, looking at the babies, it was very difficult to decide which they were.

Having given us all the details of where they lived and how they found them, the couple bade us farewell, leaving Sarah to settle the babies into a rearing tub with heated mat.

I quickly rang through to Simon King, who lives locally, and explained to him what had happened. If anyone was going to know what they were, it would be him. He had had a tame weasel as a pet for quite some time. Simon told me that if they were weasels then they would have a small disc of brown fur just under the line of the mouth, and indeed they did have. He was also able to give Sarah quite a few good hints on feeding them, so it was a very worthwhile call. The young weasels were a boy and a girl and were to be named Wilma and Wilfred.

Weasels hunt by day and night and are heavily predated by owls, foxes, birds of prey and, of course, the cat. Wildlife gets blamed so much for killing things, and yet if you add all the population numbers of mammal predators that we have in this country, it will still not reach the number of domestic cats that we have – and they kill for fun!

Although still with their eyes closed, the young weasels would take meat. They are one of the few mammals to wean before their eyes open, with their mother bringing back prey for them to eat. But they were still going to need milk feeds and it was a dedicated Sarah who, after finishing her shift at 10 p.m., went on to take them home to carry on feeding them late into the night.

I went back through to tell Derek about the unusual babies. It had been a bit of a busy evening and Derek was busy with books spread all over the kitchen table, still trying to balance some figures. I hadn't even made the bed yet so made my way through to the bedroom. The chocolate brown shadow tripped along by my feet. Despite it being nearly 11 p.m., it was still mild so I didn't bother to close the window. I pulled back the covers of the bed and started to straighten the sheet. I thought I heard a commotion outside and moved towards the window. Looking down towards the badger enclosure all seemed quiet, but as I turned to carry on with making the bed I heard the noise again.

I ran straight out of the bedroom to the kitchen, grabbing the torch. 'Quick!' I said to Derek. 'I can hear badgers fighting.'

Without questioning, Derek followed me. Collecting the keys to the badger sett from the key cupboard, we made our way down to the enclosure. The boar badger had finally made his way through the chain link and was in the observation sett. I was terrified as to how much damage he would cause, knowing full well he was capable of killing the cubs.

We switched on the lights in the observation sett to see that he had made his way through to the chamber. Meadow, Taffy and Eric were in one chamber, Ebony, David and Barley were still in the alleyway outside. Taffy was the one with blood on his ears, all the others had no apparent injuries. The boar was panting with all the effort of getting through the wire and was nervous at now finding himself in unusual surroundings. He growled and tore at the bedding in the chamber. Taffy decided to enter the chamber and fight this individual that had dared to intrude into their home. As soon as he reached the entrance, Taffy lunged at the boar.

Incredibly, all the other cubs went in to join the fight and the boar was bewildered by their actions. I ran outside and screamed for the cubs to come out. Barley and Ebony bolted straight out, followed quickly by the others, looking to me for security against their first big lesson in survival. Derek, who had followed me out, quickly jammed the board that divided the alleyway down the walls, actively separating the cubs from the boar.

'What do we do now?' he asked.

Trying to think fast, I suggested that we get a badger cage from the casualty pen and place it in front of the tunnels leading into the chambers. 'If you can go and jump up and down on the boards over the chambers, hopefully it will frighten the boar to run out into the cage and I can slide the door down before he gets the chance to turn round to get out', I suggested.

With adrenalin running, we both acted quickly, neither thinking of our own safety, more aware of the frightened cubs and a situation that needed to be dealt with. It actually went exactly to plan. Derek went to the back of the chambers with a heavy brush and banged on the boards, causing the boar to scuttle out straight into the cage that we had placed by the entrance. Slamming the door down quickly and securing it, there was no sense of achievement on my part, just the dread of what to do next.

We lifted the cage out of the alleyway and put the badger in by the casualty pens. He was sweating with fear and the effort of fighting. We covered him with a blanket and left him for a while. Derek went to mend the fence and I went to check on the cubs. Several had blood on their fur but very little damage: Taffy was the one with the bitten foot and torn ear. I changed the straw in their chambers as the cubs gambolled and played. In a period of half an hour, it had all been forgotten about. It was as if they knew the badger had been taken away and they were safe.

Checking them for the last time, although I would give them a good examination the next day, I switched out the lights. Derek joined me when he had finished the fence and put away the tools.

'What are you going to do?' he asked me quietly.

'I suppose I could ring Colin in the morning and ask him what . . .' I started.

'Oh, come on, Pauline, it's the one that attacked you – even if you ring Colin, what's he going to do?' he snapped.

It was the badger that attacked me. I would remember that face quite easily – he even had a scar on the head above one of the ears. It may have been a scar from a car accident: the animal could well have brain damage and be confused. Rightly or wrongly, I decided to put him down.

With the crush on the side of the cage, I was able to give him an anaesthetic quite easily. And the angry distressed animal slowly slipped into unconsciousness, breathing heavily.

I had no fear as I lifted him from the cage. If I could have thought of any alternative, I would have done it, and as I gently put him to sleep I cried for him as I have cried for others. Whatever he had done, ill or not, he just hadn't understood.

I have to say that I had not realised how I had worried about the cubs unconsciously, knowing that the badger had still been around. After his death, it was like a weight lifted off my shoulders. We had a vet out to check all the cubs the next day and, apart from a few minor bite wounds, bumps and bruises, they were fine. I must have picked up the first sign of fighting almost as it happened.

Sarah's baby weasels grew at a phenomenal rate and from blind helpless babies they became streaks of lightning capable of escaping from their tubs and being like quicksilver. Some hilarious and entertaining pursuits ensued, playing peek-a-boo around all the tubs on the surfaces, so it was decided to move them down to the casualty pens. First we had to block up the drainage holes as an old saying is that a weasel can go through a wedding ring (!), so you can see the security involved in keeping them captive until able to fend for themselves.

The pen was dressed with a bird box as a nest, branches and tubes and plenty of toys. The sight of a young weasel carrying a soft toy practically ten times its size shows the ability of this small mammal to kill and carry a young rabbit in times of need. They were very entertaining to watch and we needn't have worried about how we were going to release them, as they decided for themselves.

We had underestimated their climbing abilities – they soon demonstrated that they were able to climb up sheer cement block walls and escaped through the ceiling! Disappointed that their departure had not been planned, but more than happy that they would be able to fend for themselves, the drainage holes in the pen were reopened and hedgehogs were housed in the vacant pen.

Much to our amusement, we realised the next day just how adept at fending for themselves these little weasels were going to be. Having placed the food in for the hedgehogs, all you had to do was to stand back and watch for a few minutes and two little weasels would appear running along the cowshed wall. Diving under the casualty pen gate, they then ran up the drainage tubes into the pen with the hedgehogs, helped themselves to as much food as they wanted, and then departed back along the walls to their new home. It was some months before we eventually stopped seeing our little friends, who had certainly given us a lot of pleasure.

We were back to television cameras again when the BBC, with producer Sue McMillan, were filming for 'Nature Detectives'. Taffy, Meadow and crew were now ready to go down to the RSPCA and yet again the process of catching them, travelling to West Hatch, blood-testing and tattooing was all to be televised. Debbie was helping me and we both had to be miked up for most of the day. A small radio microphone is placed just under the neckline of your sweater or tee-shirt with a small pin and a thin lead goes down to a transmitter pack that is usually put in the back pocket of your trousers.

These microphones carry quite a distance and I was surprised when, in the car travelling down to West Hatch, Debbie and I were told that the sound men in the car behind could still pick up what we were saying. You tended to be fairly uncomfortable when you needed to go to the toilet, wondering to yourself just how much they could hear if by chance they still had their receivers on. The other thing that amused me was that every so often, having the microphone on all day, they sometimes shifted, so you got used to having a man, every now and then, pulling the neck of your top forward and looking down your shirt just to 'check if the microphone was still in place'. Needless to say, Debbie, who as I have mentioned before is much better endowed than me (and younger!), seemed to be checked a lot more than me!

We were to film the release of Taffy's lot in the same way as for Glade, and yet again it was a lovely site and everything went well. No air flight though – can't have it all!

I was quite pleased that all the television work was over. With only one more group to move down to grassed enclosures, soon most of our badger work would be over for that year. I inwardly groaned, therefore, when a researcher contacted me to ask if a Japanese television crew could come and film some badgers. I explained that we only had one group of cubs still to be moved in the next week, and two adults in casualty pens, one of which was a road traffic accident, the other an infected wound.

That would be fine, said the happy researcher, who went on to explain that the crew would consist of a producer, sound and cameramen – and an interpreter, as none of them could speak English. This was going to be fun, I thought to myself, and telephoned Colin to tell him the happy news.

When the film crew arrived, they were very obviously Japanese. There was plenty of bowing and handshaking and nervous laughter. The interpreter explained that most of the programmes in Japan are done in the style of a quiz show, and with each animal they like to ask viewers to ring in with some fact about the animal's lifestyle. Could I, he asked, explain briefly about badgers.

I described how the badger is a nocturnal animal that lives underground. That it is a strong animal that digs its home, called a sett, and that each badger would belong to a family with a dominant boar and a dominant sow, with as many other members of the family that the area belonging to that family, called a territory, would support in food supply. I explained that badgers relied greatly on their sense of smell, which is very much stronger than ours. That they had a musking gland at the base of the tail, with which they would constantly mark each other to create an individual smell that members of the family could be recognised by.

This was duly repeated back to the other men with great gesticulation and I could tell that he was getting to the final part when he turned his back to the producer and backed towards him, bending his knees, taking a scenting 'stance' with the exclamation of 'hoh' followed by gales of laughter. This resulted in all the men adopting this position and repeating the 'hoh' exclamation. Animated conversation resulted in deciding that this was to be what they wanted the viewers to ring in about. I decided that I was thankful that this programme was not to be televised in this country.

All very jolly, we made our way down to the casualty pens to see the badgers in care. With the lack of language, it was easier once we got there to place my finger to my mouth and say 'shhh!' in order to get them to stop jabbering. It was like a group of children, turning one to the other, finger to mouth, 'shhhing' each other! A line of Chinese (Japanese?) whispers.

Solemnly, we all crept in. Peering through the window in the casualty pen door, the experience of seeing a live badger for the first time was too much for one of them who let out a loud 'ohhhh!', which resulted in everyone else putting their fingers up

The guilty person being hit on the head with the producer's clipboard.

to their mouths again and shushing and the guilty person being hit on the head with the producer's clipboard.

Trying to retain a sense of professionalism, the producer beckoned all outside to discuss how this could be filmed without disturbing the animals. This was all repeated back to me as the producer stared severely at the guilty cameraman. They only wanted footage of them in the pens, and just to open the doors quietly for them to shoot a few seconds of the badger inside was all they required. In fact, I was soon to understand that there was a vast difference between a BBC crew and a Japanese crew.

It was one take and one take only. Goodness knows how they cut it all together, but as far as I was concerned – nice and easy. It was then time to catch up the cubs, the last group to go, in the new casualty pens. There were seven altogether, and again the interpreter explained to me that I could just go ahead and do it, they would film round me. The cubs slept in a wooden box during the day so blocking the front and opening the lid, I was able to scruff them one by one and put them in the waiting cages. These were all totally wild cubs and you do need to get a fairly strong hold on them as they wriggle and spit, not understanding what you are doing to them. When I finished a soft ripple of applause, followed by some more shushing, showed the crew's admiration for the way I had handled them!

Lifting the cages out to the car, I explained to the interpreter that it was now time to drive down to the RSPCA, which would be along the motorway. He repeated this to the crew, and then said to me that they would follow me.

Despite them being easy with their filming, time was moving on. I had promised to have the cubs down to Colin by 11 a.m., so as we joined the motorway I took the car up to 70 miles an hour. I checked the rear view mirror every so often to make sure that their white van was following me. After ten minutes I noticed that they were indicating to overtake me. I wondered why. There was a similar white car in front – surely they had not got confused as to which car they were following.

As they pulled alongside, I looked to my right to see what they were doing. To my utter astonishment, they had the side door of the van open and the cameraman was hanging out of the vehicle filming me driving the car! If a police car had seen our two vehicles going along at 70 miles an hour with a cameraman hanging out the van, we would have been shot.

I quickly looked forward, not wishing to lengthen the time that this filming of me driving would take. When they finished they dropped back behind me. Leaving the motorway we joined the A38 and made our way towards the RSPCA unit. I noticed a dead badger on the side of the road and made a mental note to stop on the way home and remove it.

When we arrived at West Hatch, the bowing and shaking of hands continued with Colin. The Japanese filmed all the health protocol and made arrangements to come back the next day as they wanted to film the badgers being put into the grassed enclosure.

As we were going back the same way, the Japanese crew assured me that they knew the way home and I went on ahead. Having reached the part of the road where the dead badger was, I parked and walked back towards the body. Suddenly a car horn hooted like crazy and I looked up to see arms frantically waving and Japanese voices excitedly shouting things at me, so I stood still waiting for their vehicle to pull up. The other drivers on this busy road must have been totally bemused.

'What are you doing?' asked the interpreter excitedly.

'Well, I'm just moving this dead badger off the road to put it in the hedgerow and allow nature to take its course', I explained. This was all duly repeated back to the producer.

'Why?' asked the producer. The interpreter asked me.

'Well,' I sighed, 'so that it won't get splattered all over the road, so that if other animals start to eat it they won't get knocked over. And so that drivers will not realise that badgers are around here, in case there are people around who go to dig them up.'

I stood as this was all imparted to the producer. Why is it that when you say a lot it interprets into a few words, but when the producer said 'why' it sounded more like a sentence!

'This', he repeated back to me, 'is wonderful television. We must film you doing this.'

So on a busy main road an excited Japanese film crew filmed me park my car, walk back, pick up a dead badger and throw it in the hedge. It made their day! They could not thank me enough, and with another ten minutes of bowing and handshaking, they again departed.

They did promise to send me a copy of the programme but it never came. It was probably just as well!

Colin rang me the next day, bemused himself.

'I don't think they understood half of what we were saying', he said, laughing. 'You know they wanted to film me putting the cubs in the pen?'

'Yes', I said.

'Well, after we had finished, the producer asked through the interpreter what happens next and I explained that now they were in the enclosure we would reduce all human contact. Someone would only go in once a day and throw in dead chicks and dog meat for them to find at night when they came out.' Then laughing, he added, 'The producer only nodded towards our domestic section, where we care for the cats and dogs, and asked if we got our dog meat from the dogs that we couldn't home. He didn't realise that by dog meat, I meant meat that we would feed dogs with!'

'Well,' I said, 'it has to go down as one of the more unusual film crews we have worked with.'

'It certainly does', said Colin.

August brought its expected hot and sunny days, and with plenty of visitors, we were kept busy just with demonstrations. One of the most popular events is the ferret racing, when those who like can have a flutter as to which ferret is going to be the first out of the brightly coloured drainpipes. A month of shorts and ice cream is a good way of describing August and, of course, it is a month when the corn is nearly ready to be harvested.

The inevitable telephone conversation took place.

'Good afternoon, Secret World', I politely answered.

'I want to take you down my corn field', drawled the gruff voice.

'Hello, Bill,' I answered, 'how are you?'

'Lonely', Bill snapped.

'Well, if you weren't such an awkward old sod, people would come and see you more often,' I quipped.

'I thought you were bringing your people out to see the damage that the badgers have done to my corn', said Bill, ignoring my last remark.

'Well,' I teased, 'seeing as I hadn't heard from you, I thought perhaps you hadn't had any damage this year.'

'No damage, no damage', said Bill, his voice rising, 'you should see . . .'

'Yes, sorry Bill, I was only teasing, when can we come out?' I asked. 'Next week, Tuesday or Wednesday evening?'

'I can't make Tuesday', said Bill.

'Alright, Wednesday it is then', I replied.

'Are we going out for a drink afterwards?' Bill hinted.

'Absolutely no point in coming out unless we do!' I replied. '7 p.m. by the London Inn, how's that?'

'Right', said Bill. 'They'll be surprised when they see it, you mark my words.'

'Well, Bill, that's what it's all about. Making people see the other side of the coin, when you have crop damage. See you Wednesday.'

'Bye', said Bill and dropped the phone down – conversation over!

Shirley Jenkins and Fred Stopps came with me the next week. They are members of our badger group and were interested in Bill's problem. Shirley often helps at the farm in many ways with fundraising. She lives in a lovely little cottage deep in the countryside with her friend June, together with their assortment of cats and dogs. Fred works as a lecturer and lives in the heart of Bridgwater. Both are of a similar age to me and hopefully would be diplomatic in their thoughts. I can remember Bill meeting a younger member of our badger group who went off on the tangent of 'you, as a farmer, are the guardian of the countryside and it is your place to take care of it so that we can enjoy it in years to come. It is your job to protect wildlife, not to kill.' I will not print Bill's reply. Whilst not always agreeing with Bill, I did feel that this young member had been slightly untactful in his way of talking to Bill.

I drove Fred and Shirley to the London Inn, to find Bill sat proudly on his old red tractor. With shirt sleeves rolled up, he was ready to take us on. As we neared the inn, Bill made his 'waggons ho!' action, which basically meant 'follow me', as he revved the tractor, causing the smoke to billow from the slim metal exhaust, and started off towards the field.

'Ohh,' said Shirley, 'he looks rather severe.'

'He can get very angry at times,' I teased, 'almost violent on occasion.'

Shirley looked at my face, not sure if I was serious or not.

Bill turned into the lane and we bumped down the track until we could go no further by car. Pulling in as close to the side of the lane as possible, I parked the car and we all got out. Bill climbed down from the tractor and leaned against it as we approached.

'So,' he mused, scratching his beard, 'you're all friends of Kidner woman, eh?'

'We certainly are', answered Shirley, having sized up that this was part of his little game. 'We've come to look at your corn field.'

'Right', said Bill, turning up towards the field; 'you won't believe the amount I've lost, I tell you, and who's going to pay, that's what I want to know.'

We all followed meekly behind and stood to survey the field once we got to the top. Fred couldn't get over the number of people up there walking their dogs.

'They shouldn't be allowed to just walk through your fields like this', said Fred, who I would imagine is a person inclined to look after his things very well. He was astonished at how many people were out with their dogs, nonchalantly walking past, many not even aware that Bill was the owner of the land.

Bill had found an ally. He quickly explained to Fred how there was a public footpath, but nobody kept to it.

'Look', Bill said to Fred, pointing to a pile of horse dung. 'Even bring horses up here.'

'No!' said Fred, quite shocked.

'Not a by your leave, just come up here, thinking they own the place . . .', Bill went on.

Shirley and I walked together behind the two men. She nodded towards Bill, 'He's found a friend!' and we laughed, but really it was no laughing matter. Besides the damage that Bill was about to show us, a lot was actually caused by members of the public not keeping to footpaths and allowing dogs off their leads to run into the corn and out again, with no thought as to the damage to the crops.

Bill explained to Shirley and Fred about the setts over in the adjoining field and pointed out the large areas of corn that had been flattened. He leaned against the fence.

'Ere!' he said, waving at me, 'I didn't tell you this, I had one of your what d'ya call it, conservationists, up here the other day. Complaining at me saying we ought to be allowed to shoot the badgers. And I said to him, "ere, come and have a look at this, if you like wildlife" and I took him over to my trailer over there and showed him some baby rabbits that have been living under there. "Hah!" he said to me, "don't talk to me about rabbits, they've been coming in and eating my lettuces in my garden." "Well", I says, "so what did you do about that?" I asked. "I shot em" he said. Now you tell me what is the difference between his lettuce and my corn?' said Bill, wagging his finger at us all. And to be fair, he had a point.

Diplomatic Shirley changed the subject. 'Let's have a picture of you, Bill, in your corn field showing all the damage, especially as you're a fine figure of a man.' (She'd got him sussed!)

Marching into the centre of the flattened corn, Bill started to undo his shirt. Shirley stood, camera ready, waiting for him to stop moving. He continued to undo his shirt down to his waist.

'Em, Bill', said Shirley, 'I just want to take a photo of . . .'

Bill reached inside his shirt and brought out a folded brown paper bag. Bemused, we all watched. Unfolding the bag, Bill reached inside and brought out . . . a comb, which he duly used to do his hair before putting it carefully back in the bag, back inside his shirt, which was duly done up. Then, completely ready, he posed for his picture. I managed to get a picture of the 'fine figure of a man' too.

We ended our evening with a drink as promised, and whilst not resolving Bill's problems, it certainly opened the eyes of a couple of members as to some of the damage that can be done to crops in the summer.

My photo, which in fact was a slide, was useful because although Bill accuses me of only talking about the 'nice side' of badgers when I give my talks, I do also talk about the problems they can cause. I was quite glad that I had included the slide when I went to a WI meeting the following month to give a talk on badgers at a village near Othery, where Bill lives.

A kind, small, elderly lady greeted me when I arrived and showed me into the hall.

'Thank you so much for coming', she said graciously. 'We've got a lovely turn-out, and are so looking forward to hearing you.' Then she dropped her voice and averted her eyes to the back of the hall. 'We're usually only ladies, but there's an elderly gentleman here who has come to listen to you as well', she whispered. 'I don't know who he is but he was sat out on the fence when the first person arrived.' She smiled nervously.

I looked around the hall at the group of ladies, and there sat at the back was Bill.

'Don't worry,' I assured her, 'I do know him!'

I had great pleasure in doing my talk especially when I came to the point of talking about crop damage, when I was able to change the slide to Bill standing in the corn damage. I think Bill was just a little bit proud of being on the screen, and so he should, looking so distinguished. But I do think that was one point to me for having included it in my talk!

But in another area, I was about to hear of a failure. In early September, Colin contacted me. He had been talking to Martin in Suffolk and they were having problems with Glade. He had got used to them going up to feed. It made no difference if they altered the pattern of feeding or used different people – if he heard someone coming, Glade was coming out of the sett wanting attention.

'I'm afraid there's nothing for it,' said Colin, 'we are going to have to catch him and bring him home. What do you want me to do? I can put him down or you can have him back.'

'I'll have him back', I said. I hadn't even thought about it, asked Derek or anything – I just couldn't bring myself to put him down.

Colin said he would let me know when it would be.

That evening, Derek and I really talked it through. If Glade came back, for my own safety in keeping a male, we would need to have him neutered which meant that he could not have his freedom in the way that Bluebell had. It would be unfair to keep him on his own, but this was not a problem as we had already been approached by someone in Kent who had a female cub that had been in a car accident. The cub had fractured its jaw which had been wired by the vet, but once healed, the teeth were no longer in line and she would be unable to forage well enough in the wild to survive, so we had already been considering giving her a home.

If Glade was to be put with her, we certainly would not want them to breed, producing more cubs in captivity. We have always been against keeping animals in captivity, but as Simon King once said to us, sometimes things are handed to you on a plate and as ambassadors of their species, animals in captivity have a role to play in education. I still worried that I was using these excuses to fulfil my own desire to have him back. Would he be happy here in captivity – would he even remember us? Glade had been away from us for three months. We would have to wait and see.

10

Mr Woo

The observation sett was given a thorough clean-out after being empty since Taffy and his crew had left. The wire in the front of the enclosure had been completely redone, so Glade's new home was ready and waiting for him when he arrived. It had been a long way back from Suffolk, so as we unloaded the carrying case with Glade inside, I wondered what his reaction was going to be.

Colin had said that it had not been a problem to catch him. They had simply taken the cage up to the site, called his name and out Glade came. It was the first time in all the years that we had had a failure, and trust it to be with this bumptious cub that had been so special. I'm sure animals are able to pick up on emotions. Perhaps Glade had understood just how important he had been to me in healing the huge gap that had been left when Bluebell had died and I could so easily have given everything up. Ironic, too, that through all the problems that we had had, out of the forty-two cubs dealt with in that season, he should be the one returning to us.

We carried his case into the observation sett and I wondered what he would be thinking: this was a place that he had never seen before. Would he even remember me?

'Do you know,' said Colin, 'he reacted as soon as we turned into the farm – he was up in his cage and looking around. Let's get him out and see what he does.'

A much bigger Glade walked out of his cage: a sleek young male, a far cry from the fourteen-week-old cub that left us in early May. One of the assistants from the RSPCA, a young man called Paul, was there also. Glade patrolled his new surroundings and then came up to the legs of Colin and then Paul. Then it was as if he had suddenly realised that I was there and he turned towards me, making the lovely purring sound of greeting that they do. Sitting on the bench, I fondled his ears. Glade put his front paws on my knees and 'preened' my jumper gently with his teeth.

'I think he's glad to be home! It's been a long journey for him,' said Colin, 'but he's back where he wants to be.'

I will never understand why Glade was a failure, why certain badgers bond far more readily with humans than others. And sometimes it has nothing to do with the amount of contact that the animal may have. Other cubs that have come in very tiny and needed constant nursing, and due to our not having another cub of the same size have been denied badger company for quite some time, have still reverted to being wild with no problem at all.

We have even had a cub that turned up starving in a garden, and the people who lived in the house eventually only brought it in because it continually kept scratching at the door – obviously relating humans with help. Perhaps this is the difference between setts that you can watch easily and others where the individuals never overcome their fear of humans, and are never seen. That in a way is what is so magical about badgers. We think we know so much, and yet we understand so little about them.

For the time being Glade settled in the observation sett on his own and we continued to make arrangements for the cub from Kent to come to us as soon as she was well enough.

With one orphan returned, it was time for another to leave me. And despite not being so pretty as the roe deer, my chocolate brown shadow was going to be one that I was going to miss dreadfully, as I had got so used to her following me all the time.

As usual it had been left to Colin to find a release site, which in itself was quite difficult. There were very few feral herds around here; most fallow deer are farmed. Eventually, through speaking to Mary-Lee, who became the new 'mum' to Dot, Colin heard of a couple who farmed fallow and would be very interested in Teddy, again as a useful member of the herd to lead them around from paddock to paddock. Their farm was a long way from the road and very safe from poachers, and they were particularly interested in Teddy as she was the lovely chocolate brown colour which, as yet, they had not had.

I did not need to see where Teddy was going. If Colin was happy with it as a new home, then I had every confidence in it. I also could not bear seeing her go and found it easier to say my goodbyes when she left our place. Time and again, when I sit in my chair in the kitchen close to tears, having yet again seen something that I loved so dearly go on to its next home, I question if it is all really worth it.

Yet later in the year, I was to visit Teddy's new home and to see the beautiful countryside that she now lives in. It may be that when she is old, she will be culled, but her death will be quick, sadly something that nature very often cannot offer. And meanwhile she has a protected life where she will have young of her own, become part of a herd that will roam freely over large areas, and enjoy life to the full.

Colin was to bring photographs the following year showing the roe deer that fleetingly revisited the paddocks, showing that Beauty had survived his first winter. He also had photographs also of the new setts that had been dug at the release sites where our families of badgers had gone to, and even pictures of the badgers themselves, now almost adults. Then you know without question that our ethics of release has to be the best way. And anyway, if we were to keep everything, soon our pens would be full and then what would happen with the orphans the following year?

The conscience of a wildlife rehabilitator is constantly tested and I found great empathy with Katherine McKeever who wrote the following article in the British Wildlife Rehabilitation Council Newsletter. This lady is from The Owl Foundation in Ontario, Canada, and she discusses the difficulty in having a love of an animal. She writes:

What can we say about 'quality of life', that has not been said before by many tongues? The problem is not in finding other words to define its meaning, the problem seems to be that the meaning itself is not endorsed by the actions of so many wildlife handlers. Why is this? Is it because we have not the convictions, clearing our thought of everything except a rational look at the quality of life available to the creature in hand?

What is it, then, that gives quality of life to wildlife? Surely the very fact of being at liberty, however briefly and precariously, the ability to make all the choices, the fulfilling of an ancient role. Included here must be the restoration of freedom when it was almost lost forever; a gift that is ours to give, a joy beyond imagining for the lucky ones. But what about the ones that are now permanently maimed, the ones for whom freedom can never come again? Ah yes, what about them? How shall we restore the quality to their lives?

Now we are in a minefield of good intentions, of the forlorn hopes that blind us to reality. Now we are in the business of nurturing that sad spark of life, mistaking it for a way of living, all the way to its lonely end.

Then is euthanasia the only answer? No, but it is usually the best answer. Think about what it is: the instant oblivion, the end to pain and terror, a compassionate and moral alternative to a life of constant stress – so diminished in quality that its maintenance is really an act of cruelty. Surely it is time for us to accept that when release is irresponsible, the chances for a life of quality in captivity are narrowed down to the very expensive for the very few. Here is an example of what should be provided, in order to justify the life maintenance of a damaged wild creature; a creature that was born free and will remember freedom all its life, a creature that will never be tame. Let us suppose it is an owl, unable to fly.

Can you provide it with an enclosure as long and as high as it should have had if it could fly? It will need that same size for its psychological health. It will need high branches, and a way to climb up to them, where it will feel safe, reducing stress. It will need arboreal pathways to all other parts of the cage, both high and low. It will need thick branches and thin branches, so it can change the grip. Some branches should incorporate leaning posts, *because it will spend its life perching or walking from now on, and even free owls like to lean against the trunk of a tree. It will need roosts that are under the open sky and roosts that have some shelter and others with a maximum shelter. It will need a wide, shallow, non-slip pool and a log or rock beside it for ablutions. It will need a lifelong diet of the natural prey items of its species. It will need the opportunity for companionship with another of its own kind, but also the ability to be alone in its own space. And it will need to be left alone, by humans. It will need every possible choice that you can think of – give it, even if you can never give it the one thing it never stops waiting for.*

If you can do all these things, then you will have reduced stress (the biggest killer of them all) to the point where your bird will never get sick, never need medication, and may even form a bond and produce offspring as it lives on to its potential lifespan. And you will be able to say, truly, that you gave it a life of quality.

But right at the beginning, there is something you should know, even if it breaks your heart. For all your long hours and physical effort, the self denial and the expense, the arguments with others over your priorities, and even your genuine affection for this creature you have come to love, there will always be one thing missing from its life. And if you leave the cage door open, it will opt for that one thing above all the others that you gave it, and it will walk out the door to freedom, and its death. Because this is the way of wild life.

The more you work with wildlife, the more you question what you should be doing. And it is never easy. Not only do you have a responsibility to the animal concerned within your care, but you also have a responsibility to the animals within the area into which you return a casualty. Are you upsetting the balance of nature – are you returning a non-viable animal back to the wild, basically causing him or her to suffer again, because you feel it is 'kinder' than to put it to sleep?

Are you even returning it to a different location from where you found it, just because you think it's a nicer place? Only a few years ago, I wrote in my book *My Secret World* about Urbie, who was found in Weston-super-Mare, in a very built-up area, and we questioned whether we should put him back. Linda was the person to release him late one night, very close to the garden where he was found. She let him go in a playing field and surprisingly, when he was released, he met up with another badger that greeted and played with him before they both ran off. We could find no trace of setts prior to releasing him and yet he was obviously returned to his social group.

Quite by chance, a few years later we discovered where the setts were, having been called out to a garden problem. It would have been so easy to have released him further out in the undeveloped area of Weston, but where he was returned to was where his home was, where he knew where to find food and water, where his own family was, even if it was a built-up area.

After a year of so many ups and downs, I tried to be positive. We needed to learn from the problems of the parvovirus incident, the health protocol needed for badgers, the absolute right that wildlife has to be given first aid, pain relief and fluid therapy by vets when taken into care, in the same way as any other domestic or farm animal, and the need to get information recorded and disseminated to vets and other wildlife workers.

Through the Bluebell Sett Clinical Studies Group, Veterinary Days for Badger Care were organised firstly in our area but with the aim of holding them throughout the country – and, indeed, in time to cover other species. I have become involved with day courses for trainee veterinary nurses and talks to students of the British Veterinary Association in London, besides other aspects of the National Federation of Badger Groups: I am a member of the Rehabilitation Working Party and the Farming and NFBG Advisory Group, as well as being involved with the TB issue. All of these things take time in addition to my involvement with badgers at home but, more importantly, it all takes money.

Over the years, the wildlife work had been financed by the attraction 'Secret World', and then the creation of the Bluebell Sett charity had helped with the costs of caring for the animals, but soon even the charity could not keep up with the costs of the national work that we were doing.

This is where Care for the Wild International (CFTWI) stepped in to help us. They had donated to our charity in the past as, indeed, they finance many projects of wildlife hospitals across the country. Immediately on hearing that we were having difficulties in financing our work, Bill and Chris Jordan, directors of this charity, came to see us to find a way in which they could help. Their charity is one that acts quickly as soon as help is needed, not only in this country but across the world. We were to be amazed at the broad spectrum of help that they have given over the years to tigers, elephants, rhinos and orangutans, to name but a few. Not many people realise that CFTWI are one of the main sponsors for Daphne Sheldrick's elephant orphanage, the Elephant Hospital in Thailand for working elephants, the Orangutan Foundation in Borneo and the Rhino Orphanage in Kenya.

Much of their work entails buying medical equipment, educating and involving local people to help care for the animals as well as buying vehicles and machinery. With equipment, it is important that they retain the ownership of everything as the lifestyles in most countries are so poor that were they given such items, these would soon be sold. But retaining ownership means that they must maintain them and regularly visit to make sure that all finances and facilities are being used to the best advantage for the animals concerned.

A great deal is also done by CFTWI in fighting for the protection of these animals at government level as there is an ever-increasing problem with the smuggling of many products from endangered species, such as ivory, bear bile and tiger bones – all now reaching higher market value than gold or drugs.

By now Glade had a family of his own in the observation sett. He had been joined by Nippy from Kent, who had suffered a fractured jaw that did not mend properly, and another female called Foxglove, who had a liver complaint and was likely to need medical attention at various times through her life. He was a very content badger with two young ladies to curl up with to sleep and for company to play with at night.

Chris and Bill came up with the suggestion of starting a 'Foster a Badger' scheme so that people could sponsor the care of Glade, Nippy and Foxglove, and any remaining money would help finance all the work that is carried out for other orphaned and injured badgers at our centre. With this same scheme of fostering tigers, rhinos and elephants, Bill and Chris for CFTWI were able to support other orphanages across the world.

This fostering scheme has been our saviour; it has enabled us to continue to care and fight for the badger. It may be that the badger does not seem so important as those other species that sound so grand. But they do need help. Many think that they are not persecuted now, with the law to protect them – some people think they are even overprotected.

Just as an example let me tell you about what happened the following year. We were to hear of a badger found by police in a van that had been stopped by them. It was coming over from Ireland to the Midlands and the police were looking for explosives. They found no explosives but hanging up in a sack bag in the back of the van was a badger. It is known that there is a trade of badgers from Ireland to the Midlands, badger baiting being a sport that is carried out undercover in several cities.

Badgers are disliked by many in Ireland and if you have the right contacts, it is perfectly possible to go on badger digging and baiting holidays in Ireland, despite this being totally illegal.

The driver of the van was to say that he had found the badger on the road and, thinking it was dead, picked it up to have it stuffed. The police doubted this story especially as the bag was tied tightly and hung up, making it impossible for a live badger to dig out of it. Why tie a bag up tightly if the badger is dead? The badger was also in the middle of the load, which in itself was suspicious.

On examination the badger was found to have a lot of soil in its fur, which is indicative of an animal that has been dug out. It was also x-rayed to see if there were any broken bones or injuries consistent with the story of being found on the side of the road as if it had been knocked down. No injuries were found – nor did the vet notice the three well-developed tiny bodies inside. While the female badger was held in care at a rehabilitation centre in Yorkshire, she was to produce three cubs.

We were contacted by the RSPCA's special operations unit, to see if we could house the sow and cubs as they wished to move her to an unknown safe location while the prosecution went ahead. So once the cubs were old enough, she was moved to us. As there were no details of where she came from, we eventually added three more cubs to her and finally, at the end of the summer, they were released as a family group in a new release site.

I am pleased to say that the driver eventually decided to plead guilty and was given a six months custodial sentence and fined £3,000. It is just so sad that so many prosecution cases, for one reason or another, never get to court.

Just as tigers are killed for many different parts of their bodies, elephants for their ivory, rhinos for their feet and their horns –

badgers are taken for their fighting ability, because they're 'good fun'.

But badgers carry bovine TB. Yes, a small percentage do and an even smaller percentage will possibly become infectious and thereby present a risk. It is incredibly naive to think that we live in a sterile world and that these odd infections crop up around us from nowhere. Disease of one form or another is ever present: salmonella is found frequently in bird droppings, and indeed we have to have some salmonella bacteria in our gut to enable us to digest our food, so a sterile world would not be a good thing. The bacterium *M. bovis* is found commonly in the soil. It only when the immune system of an animal is lowered that transmission is able to occur.

Badgers have been blamed for bovine TB in cattle for over twenty-five years, resulting in 21,000 of them being killed – eighty per cent of which were totally healthy animals. Disgracefully, hardly any data has been collected from all these dead animals. It has just been a blind slaughter which, one has to say, has not been successful in reducing the incidence of TB.

Now we have a culling programme being introduced by the government which will result in many more badgers being killed. There are many aspects of the culling programme that I have grave reservations about, but at least the animals will not be tossed on a heap as they were before. Detailed post mortems studying the carcasses will, we hope, be looking at all aspects – the very least of which is the classification of infected animals, infectious ones and those that could well be immune.

But the Ministry of Agriculture, Fisheries and Food are at last accepting that there are many factors to this complex problem. After years of indoctrinating both the veterinary profession and farmers alike, they are seeing the need for research into cattle-to-cattle transmission, animal husbandry, trace mineral element deficiency, climate, geology, and the test itself is being addressed. MAFF are looking at other wildlife, knowing full well that deer are also implicated in the disease problem, and with in-depth research other carriers may be found. Despite the NFU's stance in this matter, at last anyone with any intelligence will realise that the slogan 'go kill a badger, to make yourself feel better' is not going to bring an answer to the problem.

You need to bring the whole problem back to the fact that the only danger we have is TB in cattle. Find a vaccine, a way of boosting their immune system, or find out why it is being suppressed, and the problem is resolved.

Any thoughts of issuing licences to allow farmers to shoot badgers would open wide the possibility of persecution of the badger all over again, and all legislation to protect them will be lost. The badger, emblem of all our wildlife trusts, has to be a species most at risk through ignorance.

A very brown Simon and Nikki returned to our shores, complete with souvenirs, tons of photos and two didgeridoos. Simon's efforts at playing the didgeridoo had progressed from when he had first purchased it (when, according to Nikki, it sounded more like a cow farting) to actually being able to play it quite well – although I think it took quite a few months of practice on Simon's part and patience on Nikki's.

They both came home to live with us, Simon taking over as administrator of the Bluebell Sett charity and Nikki having landed a job as a researcher for a television production company. It makes life a lot easier to have an extra pair of hands to help out in many ways.

It sounded more like a cow farting . . .

Nikki in particular loves the animals, thinking nothing of sharing the late-night feeds, and couldn't wait for the new season of orphans to start. But it was ironic that, for one of the babies to be cared for the following season, of all people, Nikki and Simon were probably the most suitable to care for it.

I had an unexpected phone call from a past member of staff who had gone to work at another Animal Centre. They had a wide range of zoo animals, and within the park there was a group of wallabies. One of the wallabies had taken a look inside her pouch and had seen that her six-month-old baby was an albino, a baby which, therefore, would be unlikely to survive in the wild. Not wishing to waste any further time on this scrawny pink item, she evicted it from her pouch and hopped off.

The young lad who found it was not sure what to do, and the Centre as such was not set up to deal with orphans needing intensive care. Rather than put it down, he asked if he could ring me to see if we could take it, and this he was allowed to do.

I was thrilled when he rang: of course we would love to have it, says I, without having a clue as to what it would look like, how big it was or what I was even going to do with it.

'We'll pick it up as soon as we can today', I said excitedly.

It was only just past ten in the morning on a Sunday. Derek had just finished attending to the cows and had come up to change out of his overalls.

'Guess what!' I said excitedly to Derek. 'Jason has just rung, and they've got a baby wallaby that they want to find a home for.'

'Well!' said Derek, matter-of-factly, 'We're not having it and that's final.'

'But . . .' I started.

'Definitely no, what do we want a wallaby for? It's got nothing to do with wildlife. We've got animals all over the place and we certainly don't want a wallaby' he stated, throwing his overalls down on the floor. With that he was gone.

Well, I want a wallaby, I thought to myself as I pondered the situation. I had already said to Jason that we would have it and yet Derek had – well, sort of – implied that we couldn't have it.

So I bided my time and waited for Derek to come back up for a coffee and toast while he read his paper.

'I'll make the coffee', I said helpfully as he came upstairs.

Once he got settled, I started!

'I've sort of got a problem about the wallaby . . .' I said, and Derek opened his mouth ready to reiterate what he had already said; '. . . no, let me finish. I've already said to Jason that I would have it, before I said anything to you, so really, I've committed myself.'

The second line of defence, as far as Derek was concerned, took place. 'Well, we're not keeping it; if it survives, it will have to go and live with other wallabies', he said.

'No, I agree', I said. And I couldn't wait to get downstairs because I knew that Len and Yvonne were down there. Len and Yvonne have become volunteers and are prepared to help us in all ways, even just collecting casualties. They are both in their fifties and enjoy doing a lot of travelling on their motorbike (although not with wildlife casualties!). We came to know them through their own love of badgers. They actually have badgers visiting their garden every night, although it is surprising that their badgers bother to keep coming back as Len has great fun putting their food in all manner of containers, just to see whether they can work out how to get the food from inside!

Len and Yvonne, and John and Doreen – their friends – all came to an evening buffet at Secret World and have been commandeered into all kind of jobs for us ever since.

'Len,' I said enquiringly, 'are you doing anything today?'

'Go on,' said Len, 'I can tell you want something just by the tone of your voice!'

I explained about the baby wallaby and without hesitation they were both prepared to go and fetch him for me. In fact, they rang John and Doreen, who went down with them. We gave them a box and some towels in it and off they went.

Going back into the house, I searched through my books. Derek said that wallabies weren't British wildlife but I thought there was something about them in the *British Mammal Book*. Simon and Nikki were away for the weekend, but I was sure they were going to be able to tell me all about them, and I knew that whilst in Australia, they had actually met someone who rescued baby wallabies.

The only wallabies in this country are ones that have escaped from zoos. There is a fairly small group of them in the Peak District National Park and another small population of them in Sussex. Other than that, there are a few individuals that have escaped at various times. Eating grass and bracken and especially

189

liking heather, they are capable of surviving in our countryside although they do not seem able to withstand very cold winters.

I was to read that the baby wallaby is formed for only ten days before it is born, and it then climbs up the mother's fur and into the pouch, attaching itself to the nipple. Jason had said that this one that was coming to us was just starting to poke his head out of the pouch, so they thought it was about six months old. They do not normally leave the pouch until they are nine months old and, even then, will continue to suckle until they are nearly twelve months old, so I really did not know what to expect.

Mr Woo

When 'Wally', as he was nicknamed, arrived, he was nothing like how I had imagined. I have to be honest and say that he was probably the ugliest thing I have ever seen. He was completely pink with red eyes; Jason had warned me that his fur might not grow at all but nothing had quite prepared me for this vision! Poor old Wally was very cold so we immediately turned the incubator on and rested him on a fleece.

This little animal looked just as if someone had stuck all bits of other animals together. Wally had ears like a piglet, bright red eyes and a nose like the muzzle of a horse. His tail was very long and looked like a rat's, and his feet already looked like the legs of an enormous chicken with three toes: one big toe in the middle and two side toes, one of which had two claws on – we were to learn that this was his grooming claw and also one that he was to suck like a baby sucks its thumb!

Looking very sorry for himself, Wally was very poorly, and we left him to sleep in the warmth of the incubator. Despite his looks, Yvonne and Len were to become very attached to him and in future months were often to be 'foster parents' when Nikki or I were unable to look after him.

Taking Wally out of the incubator a couple of hours later, I sat him on a towel on my lap and toileted him in the assumption that he would be the same as most babies; and indeed, as soon as I started to wipe him with a wet cloth, he urinated. Once cleaned, he was quite prepared to take a feed from the syringe. He was about 8 inches from the tips of his ears to his bottom, but if he stretched his legs they were about 15 inches long. He was so ugly, he was almost adorable – like an ET!

Well, as soon as Nikki came home and saw him, Wally became Mr Woo. A kangaroo is called a roo, so it makes sense that a wallaby would be a woo! Mr Woo became stronger every day and progressed from his incubator to a shopping bag with an electric blanket and fleece inside. He has to be one of the easiest babies I have ever cared for – he never soiled his bag and when he needed feeding, would make a strange noise like a hiccup!

Derek remained non-committal as to Mr Woo's endearing qualities, only being prepared still to voice the opinion that it would be unfair to keep him on his own as he got older. To which we all agreed – Nikki already having found sources of other wallabies so that we could try to get a mate for him. But even Simon, not a man to be seen caring for a baby, became a common sight with Mr Woo in his knapsack on his back.

A local photographer came and took a picture of Mr Woo jumping around our lounge, and all of a sudden there was a media madness as not only the local papers but the nationals, and television, including German television, wanted to come and take pictures. All of a sudden Simon, much to his disgust, had to become an agent for an albino wallaby! Pictures of Mr Woo went out in the *Daily Mail*, *The Times*, a German paper and even the *Brisbane Times* in Australia. Mr Woo even got to be on 'Blue Peter' and has his own Blue Peter Badge on the side of his bag.

. . . and kick the door if he wants to come in.

Mr Woo has had the last laugh because, originally famous for his ugliness, he has now grown an incredibly fluffy white coat and is very handsome. He can master the staircase and kick the door if he wants to come in!

Yes, this is a crazy house – where else would you find a badger asleep behind a chair, a wallaby hanging up on the door knob, and three baby robins trilling under a heat lamp by the fridge as four people – Derek, Simon, Nikki and myself – sit eating tea as if it is the most natural thing in the world.

Secret World is more than just a crazy house, it is a centre where the love of animals means that all manner of people are prepared to play a part. Maybe they are visitors that come on a regular basis and support our cause, maybe it is people who donate money or belong to the charity, or sponsor a badger. There are people willingly prepared to give up time to fund-raise, volunteers who will look after animals, men offering to do maintenance work, artists that paint our beautiful display boards, and last, but by no means least, dedicated staff who work endless hours, all hopefully for the same cause.

The work that we do to care for orphaned and injured animals is really like putting a sticking plaster over a huge wound. We make no real difference to the world but we reduce suffering, and hopefully by touching other people by the way that we work, giving talks, offering the opportunity to see things that one rarely gets to see, we endeavour to make people understand the importance of our countryside.

It must be there for animals to be returned to, a healthy balance of farming and wildlife. A countryside for future generations to enjoy, and that will only happen if we all care. I would like to thank everyone who helps us in so many ways – we would be lost without them, and you for reading this book and becoming part of our 'World'.

Britain's Badgers Need Your Help!

The lucky ones are found and cared for at the Bluebell Sett charity, Pauline Kidner's Rescue Centre.

The unique centre offers the expertise and specialised care which injured and orphaned badgers need. Each new arrival joins a family group, with whom it will eventually return to the wild.

Why Not Foster Glade, Nippy and Foxglove?

Sadly, some of the badgers never recover their independence and will always need human care. Glade, Nippy and Foxglove can't return to the wild, but they enjoy a full and happy life as permanent residents at the centre. They act as ambassadors for the species and because of them, many people learn to love badgers and to care about their plight.

Care for the Wild International's support for Pauline's work has culminated in them joining forces with Bluebell Sett and they have helped take some of the strain by running a foster programme for Bluebell Sett.

By becoming a foster parent to Glade, Nippy and Foxglove, you can help to provide the care they need. You are also helping to return young orphaned badgers back to the wild, where they belong. Your donation will provide veterinary care, rehabilitation units, food and round-the-clock care.

The foster pack includes a personalised fostering certificate; 'Badgers in My Kitchen' – a video showing Pauline Kidner's fascinating work; a badger factsheet; a photograph of the orphans; a window sticker and an update after six months of fostering, all for just £24.95.*

If you would like to become a foster parent to Glade, Nippy and Foxglove, whom you have just read about, please contact:

**Care for the Wild International
1 Ashfolds, Horsham Road
Rusper, West Sussex RH12 4QX
Tel: (01293) 871596   Fax: (01293) 871022
E-mail: cftw@fastnet.co.uk**

* Price correct at time of printing.

Bluebell Sett

Bluebell Sett is a charity with three aims:

- The rescue and rehabilitation of injured or distressed wildlife (badgers, foxes, bats, deer, birds . . .) and their return to the wild.
- To spread the message about the value of wildlife to our society.
- To add to the still very limited store of knowledge about wildlife illnesses and their treatment, which is desperately needed by vets and wildlife carers.

Bluebell Sett was founded in 1992 to support Pauline Kidner's work helping wildlife, and became a registered charity in 1995. Its name honours 'Bluebell', one of the first cubs reared by Pauline.

Bluebell Sett is run entirely by volunteers, though most of the care work is undertaken by professional staff. By becoming a member of Bluebell Sett, you can enjoy the wildlife information in the membership pack and the regular newsletters. You can also join in the events organised by Bluebell Sett, help with the fundraising or assist with wildlife care.

Some members give talks to organisations interested in learning more about wildlife. The Bluebell Sett Clinical Studies Group gathers and distributes information on wildlife diseases and their treatment to vets and wildlife carers.

Bluebell Sett run a Sponsor-a-Species programme which has been developed to help provide a year's feed and medical care for a species of animal of your choice. Sponsor-a-Species starts from only £10 per year.

If you would like further details about becoming a member or sponsoring a species, please contact:

Bluebell Sett,
Secret World, New Road,
East Huntspill,
Highbridge,
Somerset TA9 3PZ
Tel: (01278) 783250   Fax: (01278) 793109

Charity No. 1048323